Contributions to Management Science

The series *Contributions to Management Science* contains research publications in all fields of business and management science. These publications are primarily monographs and multiple author works containing new research results, and also feature selected conference-based publications are also considered. The focus of the series lies in presenting the development of latest theoretical and empirical research across different viewpoints.

This book series is indexed in Scopus.

Veland Ramadani • Wassim J. Aloulou •
Mohammad Zainal
Editors

Family Business in Gulf Cooperation Council Countries

Editors
Veland Ramadani [ID]
Faculty of Business and Economics
South East European University
Tetovo, North Macedonia

Wassim J. Aloulou [ID]
College of Economics and Administrative Sciences
Al Imam Mohammad Ibn Saud Islamic University
Riyadh, Saudi Arabia

Mohammad Zainal
College of Business Administration
Kuwait University, Sabah Al Salem University City
Kuwait, Kuwait

ISSN 1431-1941   ISSN 2197-716X (electronic)
Contributions to Management Science
ISBN 978-3-031-17261-8   ISBN 978-3-031-17262-5 (eBook)
https://doi.org/10.1007/978-3-031-17262-5

© The Editor(s) (if applicable) and The Author(s), under exclusive license to Springer Nature Switzerland AG 2023

This work is subject to copyright. All rights are solely and exclusively licensed by the Publisher, whether the whole or part of the material is concerned, specifically the rights of translation, reprinting, reuse of illustrations, recitation, broadcasting, reproduction on microfilms or in any other physical way, and transmission or information storage and retrieval, electronic adaptation, computer software, or by similar or dissimilar methodology now known or hereafter developed.

The use of general descriptive names, registered names, trademarks, service marks, etc. in this publication does not imply, even in the absence of a specific statement, that such names are exempt from the relevant protective laws and regulations and therefore free for general use.

The publisher, the authors, and the editors are safe to assume that the advice and information in this book are believed to be true and accurate at the date of publication. Neither the publisher nor the authors or the editors give a warranty, expressed or implied, with respect to the material contained herein or for any errors or omissions that may have been made. The publisher remains neutral with regard to jurisdictional claims in published maps and institutional affiliations.

This Springer imprint is published by the registered company Springer Nature Switzerland AG
The registered company address is: Gewerbestrasse 11, 6330 Cham, Switzerland

To my late grandfather Demirali, who did business with people from this region at a young age
Veland Ramadani

To my father Jalloul and my mother Moufida, my wife Ines and my children Yosr and Khalil. Thank you for your supports, all!
Wassim J. Aloulou

To anyone who did something good for me
Mohammad Zainal

Foreword

Over our respective careers, we have read, reviewed, and written manuscripts and decision letters for hundreds of business management research contributions. In every case, we would like to see the extent to which the manuscript at an individual level and the volume as a package offer a distinguished contribution. As research on family business continues to grow across the world and the majority of young businesses in the GCC region, it is pertinent to explore whether or not family businesses across the GCC region have the same peace and downfalls. The present volume includes contextual synthesis action from six GCC countries individually and lessons on the discipline to combat and vacillate. The real impact this book is looking to give, as well as the implications for students, academic scholars, and practitioners, will certainly contribute to concretely broadening the debate on the knowledge and entrepreneurial ecosystem of family businesses across the globe.

College of Healthcare Management and Economics
Gulf Medical University,
Ajman, UAE

Sudhir Rana

Editorial Board

Aidin Salamzadeh, University of Tehran, Tehran, Iran
Baker Alserhan, Princess Sumaya University for Technology, Jordan
Gadaf Rexhepi, South East European University, North Macedonia
Grisna Anggadwita, Telkom University, Indonesia
Jafar A. Haji, Kuwait University, Kuwait
Khaula Abdulla Saif Al Kaabi, United Arab Emirates University, United Arab Emirates
Léo-Paul Dana, Dalhousie University, Canada
Mehmet Bağış, Sakarya University of Applied Sciences, Turkey
Ramo Palalić, Sultan Qaboos University, Oman
Suaad Jassem, Al Zahra College for Women, Oman
Sucheta Agarwal, GLA University, India
Shqipe Gerguri-Rashiti, Universum College, Kosovo

Contents

Family Business in Gulf Cooperation Council Countries: Introductory Aspects 1
Veland Ramadani and Mohammad Zainal

Family Business in Bahrain 13
Ramo Palalić, Mohamed Rezaur Razzak, Said Al Riyami, Léo-Paul Dana, and Veland Ramadani

Family Business in Kuwait 33
Veland Ramadani, Vladimir Dzenopoljac, Mohammad Zainal, and Aleksandra Dzenopoljac

Family Business in Qatar 53
Aidin Salamzadeh and Léo-Paul Dana

Family Business in Oman 67
Mohammad Rezaur Razzak, Ramo Palalić, and Said Al-Riyami

Family Business in Saudi Arabia 91
Wassim J. Aloulou and Riyadh Alshaeel

Family Business in the United Arab Emirates 121
Luan Eshtrefi

Family Business in Gulf Cooperation Council Countries (GCC): Toward the Future 143
Wassim J. Aloulou

About the Editors

Veland Ramadani is a Professor of Entrepreneurship and Family Business at Faculty of Business and Economics, South-East European University, North Macedonia. His research interests include entrepreneurship, small business management, and family businesses. He authored or co-authored around 180 research articles and book chapters, 12 textbooks, and 22 edited books. He has published in *Journal of Business Research, International Entrepreneurship and Management Journal, International Journal of Entrepreneurial Behavior and Research,* and *Technological Forecasting and Social Change*, among others. Dr. Ramadani has recently published the co-authored book Entrepreneurial Family Business (Springer). Dr. Ramadani is co-Editor-in-Chief of *Journal of Enterprising Communities* (JEC). He has received the Award for Excellence 2016—Outstanding Paper by Emerald Group Publishing. In addition, Dr. Ramadani was invited as a keynote speaker in several international conferences and as a guest lecturer by President University, Indonesia, and Telkom University, Indonesia. During 2017– 2021, he served as a member of Supervisory Board of Development Bank of North Macedonia, where for 10 months acted as Chief Operating Officer (COO), as well. In 2021, in the study conducted by Stanford University (USA), he was ranked among the Top 2% of the most influential scientists in the world.

Wassim J. Aloulou is an Associate Professor at the College of Economics and Administrative Sciences at Imam Mohammad Ibn Saudi Islamic University, Riyadh, KSA. He received his Ph.D. in Management Sciences from the University of Pierre Mendes, France Grenoble 2, France, and from the Faculté des Sciences Economiques et de Gestion de Sfax, Tunisia in 2008. He teaches graduate and undergraduate courses on entrepreneurship in MBA and BBA programs. His research interests currently focus on digital entrepreneurship, FinTech, entrepreneurial intentions, and orientations of individuals and organizations. He has authored and co-authored multiple articles in reputable international journals (e.g., *European Journal of Innovation Management, Journal of Small Business and Enterprise Development, International Journal of Logistics Management, Journal of Entrepreneurship in Emerging Countries*, among others), books with IGI Global on *Business Transformations in the Digital Era* and on *Entrepreneurship and Organizational Resilience during Unprecedented Times*, and multiple book chapters on incubation, social entrepreneurship, women's economic empowerment, and entrepreneurial and business contexts (with Edward Elgar, IGI Global, and World Scientific publishers).

Mohammad Zainal is Professor of Applied Statistics at the College of Business Administration, Kuwait University, teaching Business Statistics and Computer Courses. He is also the current Dean of the College, and the Chair of the Board of Trustees at the Center of Excellence in Management. Mohammad's research interests include Parametric Estimation in the Skew-Symmetric Distributions, Optimization in High Dimensions, Goodness-of-Fit and Nonparametric Estimation, and the Application of Computer Methodologies to facilitate "Real-World" Solutions to Complex Business problems. Also, his research involves providing Applied Problem-Solving in Operations Strategies in SMEs and Innovation Orientation and Performance of Family Businesses. He has published in the *Journal of Family Business Management, Journal of Enterprising Communities: People and Places in the Global Economy, Frontiers in Immunology, Sustainability 2022, Periodicals of Engineering and Natural Sciences*, and the *International Journal of Business and Globalisation*.

Family Business in Gulf Cooperation Council Countries: Introductory Aspects

Veland Ramadani and Mohammad Zainal

Abstract This chapter provides introductory information about the Gulf Cooperation Council (GCC) countries, their contexts, family business in these countries, and a brief description of the chapters included in this book.

1 The context

The Gulf Cooperation Council (GCC) was established on May 25, 1981, as an intergovernmental, political, and economic union of several Arab countries, such as Bahrain, Kuwait, Oman, Qatar, Saudi Arabia, and the United Arab Emirates (Exhibit 1). As per 2021 data, the total population of GCC countries is 65,507,000 people, with a density of 21.13/km². The total area of GCC countries is 2,673,108 km², where only 0.6% is a water area. The greatest country is Saudi Arabia with 34,218,169 people and 2,149,690 km², while the smallest is Bahrain with 1,569,439 people and 780 km² (Aloulou & Al-Othman, 2021; Palalić et al., 2021).

The GCC union was created "to share common cultural values and benefits, which are based on Islamic beliefs" (Dana et al., 2021, p. 3). All GCC countries are organized as monarchies, where Bahrain, Kuwait, and Qatar are considered as constitutional monarchies, Oman and Saudi Arabia as absolute monarchies, while the United Arab Emirates (UAE) as a federal monarchy, which is consisted of seven states, and very state is ruled by its own emir (Bianco, 2020). The flag of GCC countries is presented in Exhibit 2. The flag includes on it the logo of the council as well. The logo includes the *Bismillahi-Rahmani-Rahim* phrase, which means "In the

---

V. Ramadani (✉)
Faculty of Business and Economics, South East European University, Tetovo, North Macedonia
e-mail: v.ramadani@seeu.edu.mk

M. Zainal
College of Business Administration, Kuwait University, Sabah Al Salem University City, Kuwait City, Kuwait
e-mail: zainal@cba.edu.kw

© The Author(s), under exclusive license to Springer Nature Switzerland AG 2023
V. Ramadani et al. (eds.), *Family Business in Gulf Cooperation Council Countries*, Contributions to Management Science,
https://doi.org/10.1007/978-3-031-17262-5_1

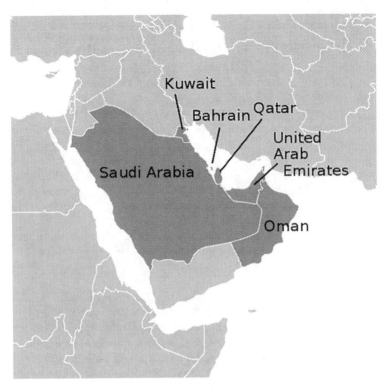

Exhibit 1 Map of GCC countries. *Source:* This file is licensed under the Creative Commons Attribution-Share Alike 4.0 International license

Exhibit 2 The flag of the Gulf Cooperation Council

name of God, the Merciful, the Compassionate," and the full name of the council, written in Arabic. The logo contains the brown-colored map of the GCC countries also, included in a hexagonal shape, which represents the six council members.

Family Business in Gulf Cooperation Council Countries: Introductory Aspects

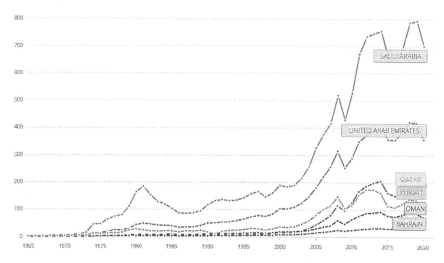

Fig. 1 GDP (current US$) of GCC countries (1965–2020). *Source:* World Bank

Headquarters of the council is located in Riyadh, Saudi Arabia. As official language is Arabic in all GCC members. Each country uses its own currency, where Bahrain uses Bahraini Dinar (BHD), the UAE uses Emirati Dirham (AED), Kuwait uses Kuwaiti Dinar (KWD), Omani uses Omani Rial (OMR), Qatar uses Qatari Riyal (QAR), while Saudi Arabia uses Saudi Riyal (SAR).

The GCC countries are generally characterized by rapid development (Dana et al., 2022). According to Dana et al. (2021), there are several reasons for this development, such as "free movement of people, goods, and capital ensured this region very fast development. The region has been of interest to investors and venture capitalists for several decades. It is known for incredible developments where the whole world comes together. The main reason for development of this region is the discovery of oil. Although the GCC members were late in discovering this precious resource, they used it for their rapid development. The first oil discovery was in Iran in 1908, then in Iraq in 1927 (although they are both not in the GCC). The first GCC member who found oil was Bahrain in 1931, then the KSA and Kuwait in 1938, Qatar in 1940, while the UAE in 1958, and Oman 1962" (pp. 3–4).

The GDP of GCC countries in 2020 was around 1418 billion USD (Fig. 1). The data for respective countries are presented in Table 1.

In the last decade, all GCC countries are working intensively on transformation and diversification strategies of their respective economies (Alharthi, 2019). For example, they have developed detailed programs and strategies for this development, such as Saudi Vision 2030, Kuwait Vision 2035, Bahrain Economic Vision 2030, Qatar National Vision 2030, Oman Vision 2040, while the UAE has developed several national initiatives such as UAE Vision 2021 and UAE Centennial 2071.

Generally, these programs and initiatives are focused on (Santosdiaz, 2020):

Table 1 GDP (current US$) of the respective GCC countries in 2020

Country	GDP (current US$/thousands)
Bahrain	34,729,228.72
Kuwait	105,960,225.69
Oman	73,971,391.42
Qatar	144,411,363.35
Saudi Arabia	700,117,873.25
United Arab Emirates	358,868,765.17
Total	**1418,058,847.60**

Source: World Bank

Exhibit 3 Downtown Dubai. *Source:* Roshan Rajopadhyaya from Pixabay (*Note:* Free for commercial use)

- *Economic sectors diversification*—The GCC countries are working on creating economies that will not rely on just one sector (e.g., oil), but on various economic sectors, such as transportation, tourism, finance, tech, and fintech.
- *Innovation and entrepreneurship*—Authorities are tailoring special programs that promote and support creativity, innovation, and entrepreneurship in order to provide opportunities, especially to young people, to develop their own businesses.
- *Digital transformation*—The GCC countries are investing huge amounts on digitalization of business processes and creation of the proper infrastructure. COVID-19 gave even more impetus to this process and justified the importance of the technology nowadays.
- *Job creation and economic growth*—Most of the strategies are focused on job creation and economic growth as the main pillars of economic development.

Considering that most of these different national programs and strategies have already started to be implemented in the GCC, even before "2030 Visions," the successes in the context of economic development and diversification are more than evident. Here we could single out Downtown Dubai (Exhibit 3), Dubai International Airport (DXB), Dubai International Financial Centre (DIFC), Smart Dubai 2021, Abu Dhabi Global Markets (ADGM), Ferrari World (Exhibit 4), Fintech Saudi, DIFC Fintech Hive, Bahrain Fintech Bay, Qatar Fintech Hub, etc.

Exhibit 4 A pan-sharped multi-spectral image of Ferrari world in Abu Dhabi. *Source:* Emirates Institution for Advanced Science and Technology/Wikimedia Commons, the free media repository

2 Family Business in GCC Countries

Family businesses, all over the world, play an important role in the economy and society (Ramadani et al., 2020). Their importance is identified in the GCC countries as well. Around 75% of active private businesses in GCC are family businesses, while 60% of them are considered as young businesses, established in the 1970s (AT Kearney, 2010). The majority of family businesses operate in retailing and trading, financial services, real estate, construction, and engineering; very few of them operate in media and transportation (Fig. 2). According to Purfield et al. (2018), 60% of the GCC's gross domestic product (GDP) is contributed by family businesses. These businesses employ more than 80% of the labor force in the region. Al-Abdel et al. (2017) noted that family businesses make up 90% of the private sector in the UAE and Saudi Arabia.

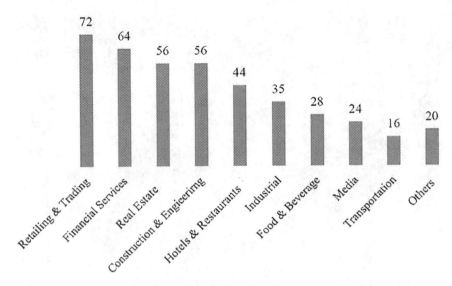

Fig. 2 Percentage of family businesses in respective sectors. *Source:* Darwish et al. (2020)

Family businesses in GCC countries are characterized by low survival rates in GCC, where the average life of these businesses is around 23 years (Al-Barghouthi, 2016). According to Darwish et al. (2020), the main reasons for the short life cycle of the family businesses in GCC are the following: increased market rivalry, lack of competitiveness, weak leadership of succession process, lack of trust among family members, insufficient resources to meet and balance the business and family needs and resistance to change. Ali and Ali (2018) found that around 70% of family businesses in GCC countries struggle to pass the business to the second generation and most of them are sold before this generation takes them over. As cited in Darwish et al. (2020), based on the data from the Family Business Institute, "only 30% of families live in the second, 12% in the third, whereas only 3% in the fourth and after generation" (p. 10). The TOP 20 family businesses in GCC countries are presented in Table 2.

Table 1 shows that Saudi Arabia dominates the TOP 20 list, with nine entries. The UAE follows with five family businesses; Kuwait is next with four family businesses in the list. This Forbes ranking is done based on several criteria, such as Group investments in regional and global stock exchanges and real estate assets; Business diversification and the number of sectors in which they have significant operations; Types of business activity and to what extent they have been affected by this crisis; Number of employees; Number of countries they are present in and geographical diversification; and Date of the establishment.

Table 2 TOP 20 family businesses in GCC countries

Rank	Company	Country	Establishment	Chairperson
1	Al-Futtaim Group	UAE	1930	Abdullah Al Futtaim
2	Olayan Group	Saudi Arabia	1947	Hutham Olayan
3	Majid Al Futtaim	UAE	1992	Michael Rake
4	Rashed Abdul Rahman Al Rashed & Sons Group	Saudi Arabia	1950	Abudlaziz Al Rashed
5	Abdul Latif Jameel	Saudi Arabia	1945	Mohammed Abdul Latif Jameel
6	Al-Ghurair	UAE	1960	Abdul Aziz Abdulla Al Ghurair
7	Alghanim Industries	Kuwait	1932	Kutayba Y. Alghanim
8	Al Ghurair Group	UAE	1960	Abdul Rahman Saif Al Ghurair
9	Zamil Group Holding	Saudi Arabia	1920	Khalid A. Al-Zamil
10	Al Muhaidib Group	Saudi Arabia	1943	Sulaiman Al Muhaidib
11	Yousuf M.A. Naghi & Sons Group	Saudi Arabia	1911	Mohammed Yousuf Naghi
12	Al Nahla Group	Saudi Arabia	1996	Abdulrahman Hassan Sharbatly
13	Alshaya Group	Kuwait	1890	Mohammed Al Shaya
14	E. A. Juffali & Brothers	Saudi Arabia	1946	Khaled Al Juffali
15	S.S. Lootah Group	UAE	1956	Saeed Bin Ahmed Al Lootah
16	Suhail Bahwan Group	Oman	1965	Suhail Bahwan
17	M.A. Al-Kharafi & Sons	Kuwait	1956	Fawzi Al-Kharafi
18	Morad Yousuf Behbehani Group	Kuwait	1935	Ali Morad Behbehani
19	Sedco Holding	Saudi Arabia	1976	Saleh Salem Bin Mahfouz
20	Zubair Corp	Oman	1967	Rashad M. Al Zubair

Source: Forbes Middle East (2022)

3 Structure of the Book

The book "Family Business in Gulf Cooperation Council Countries" is consisted of 8 chapters. This first chapter, *Family business in Gulf Cooperation Council Countries: Introductory aspects*, written by Veland Ramadani and Mohammad Zainal, provides a general overview of the GCC context and family businesses in this region.

Chapter 2, *Family business in Bahrain*, is written by Ramo Palalić, Mohamed Rezaur Razzak, Said Al Riyami, Léo-Paul Dana, and Veland Ramadani. This chapter shed light on business environment and family business in Bahrain. In this chapter, the authors provide valuable facts about the business ecosystem in the country and family businesses in Bahrain, focusing on their abilities, possibilities, participation, and contribution to the socio-economic development of the country. The final section of this chapter emphasizes the current status of family businesses and their future perspectives.

Chapter 3, *Family business in Kuwait*, is written by Veland Ramadani, Vladimir Dzenopoljac, Mohammad Zainal, and Aleksandra Dzenopoljac. This chapter discusses important characteristics of family business in Kuwait, by looking into the links between entrepreneurship, small and medium-sized enterprises, family businesses, and their growth over the years. The authors start by giving a general overview of Kuwait's business ecosystem, which served as predominant external factor for the development of successful family businesses. One of the key factors in family business development in Kuwait was the economic growth of the country after the oil discovery. Many family businesses were driven by this growth. Besides this, the tribal and family linkages were identified as an important driving force. Lastly, the chapter identifies the most successful family businesses in Kuwait and tries to assert the major common characteristics of these companies.

Aidin Salamzadeh and Léo-Paul Dana are the authors of Chap. 4, *Family business in Qatar*. The authors noted that leading families of these countries dominate the public, private, and third sectors, and based on this, they will lead most socio-economic activities. Qatar is a leading country in terms of managing public and private sectors by families. Therefore, this chapter investigates the general business ecosystem of the country and then further discusses the dominant families and family businesses in Qatar. It also provides more details about the dynamics of Qatari family businesses, and the chapter concludes with some remarks for policymakers and practitioners. Besides, it suggests some directions for future research about family businesses in Qatar.

Chapter 5, *Family business in Oman*, is authored by Mohammad Rezaur Razzak, Ramo Palalić, and Said Al-Riyami. In this chapter, the authors examine the existing academic literature as well as non-academic publications from dependable sources such as reports from international consulting firms, to compile a nuanced analysis of how Omani family businesses are different in many ways because of the idiosyncratic cultural context of Oman. An overview about the Sultanate of Oman and the business ecosystem is presented. The subsequent sections elaborate on the idiosyncrasies of Omani family businesses along with anecdotal evidence through examples of a few Omani family businesses, both large and small. Finally, the chapter ends with concluding remarks that relate the previous discourse about family businesses to the context of Omani family businesses.

Chapter 6, *Family business in Saudi Arabia*, is written by Wassim J. Aloulou and Riyadh AlShaeel. This chapter provides an understanding of the dynamics of family business phenomenon in Saudi Arabia. Initially, the authors provide a general information about the main characteristics of the country and its performance in terms of development, growth, and value. After this part, the authors describe the family business phenomenon in Saudi Arabia, its importance, and key success factors in the GCC region, new perspectives on the phenomenon by renewing it through fostering entrepreneurship outside the family business and empowering the role of women as leaders in Saudi family business. The chapter ends with concluding remarks about how to sustain the family business phenomenon from generation to another in the country and how to pursue its contribution to its economic development and to achieve the Saudi Vision 2030.

Luan Eshtrefi authored the chapter on *Family business in the United Arab Emirates*. He noted that family businesses are the backbone of the UAE. These businesses create jobs, add economic value to countries, and are pioneers in entrepreneurship and innovation. This chapter examines why the UAE is the premier country that supports family businesses. By closer view of the business ecosystem in the UAE, the chapter provides insight into five main stakeholders that together create the most effective environment for businesses to prosper. Later, the chapter focuses attention on the characteristics of Emirati family businesses and offers some insight into succession in family businesses from one generation to another.

The last chapter, *Family business in Gulf Cooperation Council Countries: Towards the future*, written by Wassim J. Aloulou, highlights the critical weight of the GCC family businesses according to main key observers. After presenting the profile of these businesses and outlining their main characteristics, the chapter sets the main challenges of family businesses in the region and identifies the most important opportunities to seize by them in the future to sustain their businesses. Some perspectives of research are advanced for scholars and practitioners. The chapter ends with proposals for future research on these businesses in a such geographical area.

4 Conclusion

The editors and authors of this book expect that these collected chapters will provide a sizable contribution to the field of family business, primarily in terms of elucidating the relevance of this field in specific regions, such as the Gulf Cooperation Council region. Even as research on general business and entrepreneurship in GCC is increasing, research focused on family business is less developed (Abdullah, 2021; Zainal, 2022). This region has not been a focal point in the current literature related to this topic and this book aims to overcome this deficit within the literature. Taking into consideration that there have only been a few studies that have paid attention to family business centered in GCC countries, this book is considered to be very welcomed by researchers all over the world and by those who are interested to know more about family business in GCC countries.

References

Abdullah, N. M. (2021). Family entrepreneurship and banking support in Kuwait: Conventional vs Islamic banks. *Journal of Family Business Management, 11*(3), 313–331.

Al-Abdel, F. S., Jabeen, F., & Katsioloudes, M. (2017). SMEs capital structure decisions and success determinants: Empirical evidence from the UAE. *Journal of Accounting, Ethics and Public Policy, 18*(2), 248–273.

Al-Barghouthi, S. (2016). Passing the Torch, family business succession, case study, Bahrain. *International Journal of Business and Management, 5*(1), 279–294.

Alharthi, M. (2019). Determinants of economic development: A case of Gulf Cooperation Council (GCC) countries. *International Journal of Economics and Finance, 11*(11), 12–18.

Ali, M. Z., & Ali, S. M. (2018). Why are family owned businesses unable to sustain beyond the second generation? *Global Management Journal for Academic & Corporate Studies, 8*(2), 128–143.

Aloulou, W. J., & Al-Othman, N. (2021). Entrepreneurship in Saudi Arabia. In Dana et al. (Eds.), *Entrepreneurship in the Gulf Cooperation Council Region: Evolution and Future Perspectives*. World Scientific Publishing.

AT Kearney. (2010). *Family business in the GCC: Putting your house in order*. A.T. Kearney, Inc.

Bianco, C. (2020). The GCC monarchies: Perceptions of the Iranian threat amid shifting geopolitics. *The International Spectator, 55*(2), 92–107.

Dana, L. P., Salamzadeh, A., Ramadani, V., & Palalić, R. (Eds.). (2022). *Understanding Contexts of Business in Western Asia: Land of Bazaars and High-Tech Booms*. World Scientific Publishing.

Dana, L.-P., Palalić, R., & Ramadani, V. (2021). *Entrepreneurship in the Gulf Cooperation Council Region: Evolution and Future Perspectives*. World Scientific Publishing.

Darwish, S., Gomes, A., & Bunagan, V. (2020). Family Businesses (FBS) in Gulf Cooperation Council (GCC): Review and strategic insights. *Academy of Strategic Management Journal, 19*(3), 1–13.

Forbes Middle East. (2022). *Top 100 Arab family businesses in the Middle East 2020*. Accessed Jun 3, 2022, from https://www.forbesmiddleeast.com/list/top-100-arab-family-businesses-in-the-middle-east-2020-1

Palalić, R., Kahwayi, A., Eddin, H., & Ridic, O. (2021). Entrepreneurship in Bahrain. In Dana et al. (Eds.), *Entrepreneurship in the Gulf Cooperation Council Region: Evolution and Future Perspectives*. World Scientific Publishing.

Purfield, M., Finger, M. F. H., Ongley, M. K., Baduel, M. B., Castellanos, C., Pierre, M. G., Stepanyan, V., & Roos, M. E. (2018). *Opportunity for All: Promoting Growth and Inclusiveness in the Middle East and North Africa*. International Monetary Fund.

Ramadani, V., Memili, E., Palalić, R., & Chang, E. P. C. (2020). *Entrepreneurial Family Businesses: Innovation, Governance, and Succession*. Springer.

Santosdiaz, R. (2020). *Overview of the economic development strategies in the Middle East's GCC Region*. Accessed May 19, 2022, from https://thefintechtimes.com/overview-of-the-economic-development-strategies-in-the-middle-easts-gcc-region/

Zainal, M. (2022). Innovation orientation and performance of Kuwaiti family businesses: evidence from the initial period of COVID-19 pandemic. *Journal of Family Business Management, 12*(2), 251–265.

Veland Ramadani is a Professor of Entrepreneurship and Family Business at the Faculty of Business and Economics, South-East European University, North Macedonia. His research interests include entrepreneurship, small business management, and family businesses. He authored or co-authored around 180 research articles and book chapters, 12 textbooks, and 22 edited books. He has published in *Journal of Business Research, International Entrepreneurship and Management Journal, International Journal of Entrepreneurial Behavior and Research,* and *Technological Forecasting and Social Change,* among others. Dr. Ramadani has recently published the co-authored book *Entrepreneurial Family Business* (Springer). Dr. Ramadani is co-Editor-in-Chief of the *Journal of Enterprising Communities* (JEC). He has received the Award for Excellence 2016—Outstanding Paper by Emerald Group Publishing. In addition, Dr. Ramadani was invited as a keynote speaker at several international conferences and as a guest lecturer by President University, Indonesia, and Telkom University, Indonesia. During the 2017–2021, he served as a member of the Supervisory Board of Development Bank of North Macedonia, where for 10 months acted as Chief Operating Officer (COO), as well. In 2021, in a study conducted by Stanford University (USA), he was ranked among the Top 2% of the most influential scientists in the world.

Mohammad Zainal is a Professor of Applied Statistics at the College of Business Administration, Kuwait University, teaching Business Statistics and Computer Courses. He is also the current Dean of the College, and the Chair of the Board of Trustees at the Center of Excellence in Management. Mohammad's research interests include Parametric Estimation in the Skew-Symmetric Distributions, Optimization in High Dimensions, Goodness-of-Fit and Nonparametric Estimation, and the Application of Computer Methodologies to facilitate "Real-World" Solutions to Complex Business problems. Also, his research involves providing Applied Problem Solving in Operations Strategies in SMEs and Innovation Orientation and Performance of Family Businesses. He has published in the *Journal of Family Business Management, Journal of Enterprising Communities: People and Places in the Global Economy, Frontiers in Immunology, Sustainability 2022, Periodicals of Engineering and Natural Sciences,* and the *International Journal of Business and Globalisation.*

Family Business in Bahrain

Ramo Palalić, Mohamed Rezaur Razzak, Said Al Riyami, Léo-Paul Dana, and Veland Ramadani

Abstract The chapter aims to provide an overview of the family business in Bahrain's business environment. The first part of the chapter introduces readers to Bahrain by giving general information about the country. The following sections are about the economic outlook where the internal and external performance of the country are emphasized. This general economic outlook is followed by the business ecosystem established in Bahrain. After providing valuable facts about the business ecosystem in the country, the chapter next portrays the family business arena in the Kingdom, their abilities, possibilities, participation, and contribution to the socio-economic development in the country. The final section of this chapter is provided by concluding remarks on the overall economic outlook, business ecosystem, and family business findings in the Kingdom, emphasizing the current status of family businesses and their future perspectives.

1 Introduction

As one of the parts of Western Asia, the land of the Kingdom of Bahrain is rich with traces of many different civilisations and ancient colonial powers that existed and passed through this region. The consequence of these ancient civilisations and powers is diversity in religions, cultures, life styles, and businesses (Dana et al., 2022). In this light, Palalić et al. (2021a) narrated that the Gulf Cooperation Council

---

R. Palalić (✉) · M. R. Razzak · S. Al Riyami
College of Economics & Political Science, Sultan Qaboos University, Seeb, Oman
e-mail: r.palalic@squ.edu.om; m.razzak@squ.edu.om; saidalriyami@squ.edu.om

L.-P. Dana
Rowe School of Business, Dalhousie University, Halifax, Canada
e-mail: lp762359@dal.ca

V. Ramadani
Faculty of Business and Economics, South East European University, Tetovo, North Macedonia
e-mail: v.ramadani@seeu.edu.mk

© The Author(s), under exclusive license to Springer Nature Switzerland AG 2023
V. Ramadani et al. (eds.), *Family Business in Gulf Cooperation Council Countries*, Contributions to Management Science,
https://doi.org/10.1007/978-3-031-17262-5_2

(GCC) region is vital due to important factors that make people to live, do business, and have pleasant vacations.

The first factor is that the GCC had been a place of Divine Revelations (Prophets). Secondly, it is an ancient road route (the region known for trade). Thirdly, it is a place of production of oil. Fourthly, it became an important financial hub in the last few decades, and lastly, a rapid education development took place (p. 1). Among these five postulates that attribute to the region, most of them describe Bahrain's Kingdom, which is why people would like to invest, work, and live in this country.

Bahrain is one of the GCC members that is located between two seas (Gulf Sea and the Persian Gulf) whereby it has got its name in Arabic language as "البحرين" (*Al-Bahrayn*). It borders with Qatar, Saudi Arabia, and Iran (Exhibit 1). The country is a peninsula made of 33 islands having in total of 765.3km^2 (Palalić et al., 2021b). The country is landlocked by Saudi Arabia and Qatar and with Iran by sea. Bahrain is the smallest country in the GCC region. Like other countries in the GCC region, Kingdom of Bahrain is wrapped with a hot desert climate with no rivers, real mountains or forests (Palalić et al., 2021b). The capital of the Kingdom of Bahrain is Manama (Exhibit 2).

Bahrain's population in 2020 is an estimated 1.472,204 (Information & eGovernment Authority (IEGA), 2022)[1] million, whereas Bahrainis are less than half of this number while expatriates comprise more than half of that number.

When describing the Kingdom, Palalić et al. (2021b) portrayed Bahrain as a country with a rich history while its first roots can be found in a few thousand years ago. For instance, one of the first civilisation places in Bahrain and the region was knowns as Dilmun, which traces of its inhabitants were found in the last two millennia. At this time, the place was populated with early Christians until the first revelation of Islam in 640 AD. This was a turning point when many people embraced Islam and became followers of Islam (Muslims). Accordingly, the flag of Bahrain symbolizes five (5) pillars of Islam (Exhibit 3). Al-Fatih Grand Mosque is presented in Exhibit 4.

However, during Islam in Bahrain, the Kingdom retained freedom for those who declared to follow Christianity and altogether had a long happy life in which they developed common human values. After some time, in the fifteenth century, the Kingdom of Bahrain was occupied by Omanis and later by the Portuguese. Later on, the Kingdom asked Persians to protect them until the eighteenth century. Subsequently, the series of Kingdom Khalifas ruled the country successfully until now.

Like other GCC members, Bahrain is also rich with a precious natural resource, the "black gold" (oil), making the country wealthy and prosperous. The discovery of oil in the twentieth century made Gulf Cooperation Council (GCC) members very rich. This event tremendously helped develop the infrastructure of all GCC members, which made the region very attractive to foreign direct investment (FDI).

From a merciless desert where no species can survive, the country has developed into a modern, growing, and high-income nation. In the last decades, Bahrain

---

[1] Available at https://www.data.gov.bh/ accessed date 18.03.2022.

Family Business in Bahrain 15

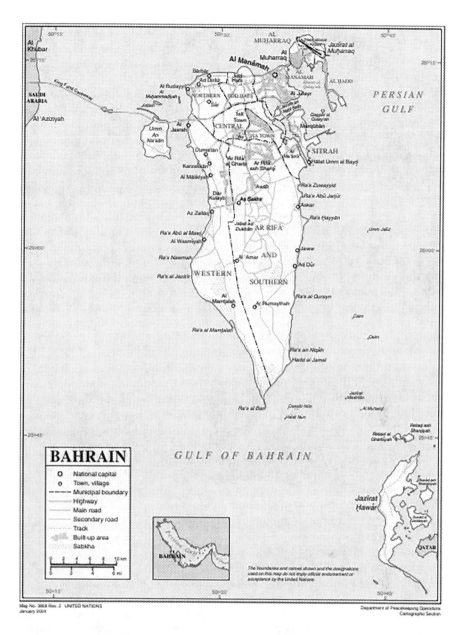

Exhibit 1 Map of Kingdom of Bahrain. *Source:* Bahrain, Map No. 3868 Rev.2, January 2004, UNITED NATIONS. United Nations. January 2004. Map No. 3868, Rev. 2. [Online]. Available at: https://www.un.org/Depts/Cartographic/map/profile/bahrain.pdf [Accessed December 2021]. Used with permission

Exhibit 2 Manama, the capital of Bahrain. *Source:* Pixabay (https://pixabay.com/photos/bahrain-night-city-night-buildings-4492669/). *Note:* Free for commercial use. No attribution required

Exhibit 3 Flag and emblem of Bahrain

became a financial hub in the Middle East (Palalić et al., 2021b), where conventional and Islamic banking and finance have been advanced and developed. Having such life and business possibilities, Bahrain opens its door to everyone willing to contribute to further development of the country in every sphere of life.

Regarding Bahrain's overall economy, it should be noted that last years were turbulent, as reflected by COVID-19. During this unmerciful turmoil, businesses around the country took their role in providing sufficient goods and services to its people. Family businesses particularly have also played an important role in overcoming issues faced with ruthless events of COVID-19 by satisfying peoples' needs, wants, and demands. As the "light could be seen at the end of the tunnel" (the end of pandemic and its global repercussions), let us have a hope that all businesses should have taken a true breath, and already continued their activities where they stopped in

Family Business in Bahrain

Exhibit 4 Al-Fatih Grand Mosque. *Source:* Pixabay (https://pixabay.com/photos/mosque-islam-faith-minaret-bahrain-1675818/). *Note:* Free for commercial use. No attribution required

the time of pandemic. Being exposed to such an event, the business environment was subject to improvements by establishing different leverages to improve the current business landscape (entrepreneurial ecosystem).

Next sections will provide more details on Bahrain's economy, the business ecosystem in Bahrain, and a general overview of family business activities wrapped up by the concluding remarks on the family business in Bahrain.

1.1 Bahrain's Economy at Glance

The national economy of Bahrain is mainly based on oil production. Other business transactions in the country were secondary for a long time. Lowering prices in oil in the last decade made the state face fiscal and external imbalances where they needed to fill the gap (World Bank-WB, 2020) at micro and macro levels.

Due to lower foreign oil prices and the spread of COVID-19, Bahrain's economy is projected to contract in 2020. It is anticipated that fiscal and external deficits will increase sharply in 2020, reversing the narrowing direction observed in 2019. Given lower oil receipts and high off-budget expenditures, the total budget deficit is expected to only steadily narrow over 2021–2022. Downside risks are triggered by the duration and depth of the two critical factors that could worsen the situation in the future, the weak oil price and the pandemic COVID-19 (WB, 2020).

Table 1 GCC countries ranking per income (GDP per capita, in $0.000)

High-income countries (GCC)	GDP per capita (in $0.000)
Qatar	63,410
United Arab Emirates	43,470
Kuwait	34,290
Saudi Arabia	22,850
Bahrain	**22,110**
Oman	15,330

Source: World Bank

In the face of more pandemic disturbances, combined with a moderate rebound in oil prices over the rest of the year of 2020, the actual gross domestic product (GDP) is projected to decline by five (5) % by the end of 2020. The growth could be bounced back to an average of two (2) % over 2021–2022, backed by infrastructure projects and non-oil activity pick-ups. The overall fiscal deficit is expected to expand to over 13% of GDP by 2020 due to lower oil prices, high budgetary expenses, and limited oil production potential. The continuation of high fiscal deficits would lead to a rapid increase in government debt, which is expected to hit 130% of GDP in 2020 (WB, 2020).

From 2000 to 2021, Bahrain's GDP Annual Growth Rate averaged 3.06 percent, with a peak of 11.43% in the fourth quarter of 2010 and a low of −9.49% in the second quarter of 2020 (Trading Economics, 2022). The duration and complexity of the twin crises of the ongoing oil price downturn and COVID-19 present downside risks. Due to reduced worldwide oil prices and the spread of COVID-19 recently, Bahrain's economy has shrunk in 2020. Accordingly, in 2020, fiscal and external deficits were predicted to climb considerably, reversing the trend seen in 2019. Given decreasing oil revenues and considerable off-budget spending, the overall budget deficit is expected to shrink between 2021 and 2022 (World Bank, 2020) gradually.

Despite all negative circumstances in the last 3 years, Bahrain is still ranked as a high-income country. However, among GCC economies, Bahrain's economy is far behind Qatar, UAE, and Kuwait, but very close to Saudi Arabia (Table 1). Oman has been qualified as the lowest high-income country among GCC members.

Regarding the world's ranking[2] of high-income economies, Bahrain is placed in 42nd place. Table 2 shows that Bahrain is among the lowest high-income countries among GCC members' economies.

According to Trading Economics (2022), Bahrain's Gross Domestic Product is composed of two industries: Goods Producing and Services Producing. The goods Producing Industry carries about 41.8% of the GDP. The most considerable portions within this industry are production (18.6%), mining (14.5%), and construction (8.1%). Services Producing Industry accounts for 58.2% of total GDP and the most prominent components in this sector are financial services (17.1%); transport

---

[2] Rankings are based on the World Bank Atlas Method using GNI per Capita (US Dollars). Source: IWA (2021).

Table 2 GCC economies ranking in comparison with the rest of the world's economies' ranking per income (GDP per capita, in $0.000)

World rank	Country (GCC)	GDP per capita (in $0.000)
8	Qatar	63,410
22	United Arab Emirates	43,470
29	Kuwait	34,290
41	Saudi Arabia	22,850
42	**Bahrain**	**22,110**
58	Oman	15,330

Source: World Bank

Table 3 Bahrain Economic Outlook

Items	2019	2020	2021 (forecast)	2022 (forecast)
Real GDP growth (%)	2.1%	−4.9%	2.6%	4.1%
Nominal GDP growth (%)	2.3%	−10.2%	9.1%	5.6%
Inflation (CPI %)	1.0%	−2.3%	1.0%	2.5%
Current account (% of GDP)	−2.1%	−9.3%	0.0%	−1.0%
Crude Oil Brent (USD)	64.0	41.7	70.4	70.2

Source: Ministry of Finance and National Economy (2022)

and communications (7.1%); wholesale & retail trade & repairs (4.5%), and real estate (3.8%).

Additionally, Trading Economics (2022) reported that in the last quarter (Q4) of 2021 the GDP's increased by 4.29%, jumping from a 2.1% growth in Q3. This was the third straight quarter of expansion in the economy, driven by a faster rise in the non-oil sector (4.21% vs 3.76% in Q3), namely electricity & water (9.59% vs 4.36%), real estate & business (4.78% vs 4.67%), and a sharp rebound in hotels and restaurants (31.66% vs −5.64%). Meanwhile, output growth has continued for transportation & communications (from 11.54% to 25.78%), agriculture & fishing (from 10.24% to 12.88%), trade (from 2.89% to 4.48%), other social & personal services (from 7.11% to 12.82%). At the same time, there was advancements in the financial sector (from −2.65% to 5.15%), and government services (from 1.89% to 3.09%). Additionally, the oil sector increased sharply (4.67% vs −4.63% in Q3). Overall, Bahrain's GDP grew by 1.49% quarterly. For 2021 full year, the economy grew by 2.22%, recovering from a sharp drop of 4.94% in 2020. In the last 20 years (2000–2021), the overall GDP of Bahrain increased from −9.49 to +4.29 (13.78%). As global issues are developing, it is expected that the GDP of Bahrain will be affected positively or negatively.

Table 3 represents Bahrain's economic outlook containing data from 2019–2021 and the forecast for 2022.

Growth in real GDP of Bahrain was noticed in 2021 (2.6%), and further development is forecasted by the end of 2022 (4.1%). Noticeably, the nominal GDP growth increased after the slowdown in 2019 and 2020 caused by the global pandemic by 2.3% and − 10.2%, respectively.

Table 4 GCC country ranking (Global Entrepreneurship Index)

Rank	Country	GDP (in $, 000)	Global Entrepreneurship Index (GEI)
22	Qatar	128	55
26	UAE	64.6	53.5
33	Oman	35.2	46.9
35	Bahrain	36.8	45.1
39	Kuwait	76	42.8
45	Saudi Arabia	49.6	40.2

Source: GEDI, Global Entrepreneurship Index (2018)

Table 5 Bahrain's ranking for GII from 2018 to 2020

No.	Year	GII	Innovation inputs	Innovation outputs
1	2020	79	63	89
2	2019	78	69	87
3	2018	72	70	74

Source: WIPO (2020)

Among other factors that make Bahrain's national economy visible and to some extent attractive (for investors) is Global Innovation Index (GII).

Global entrepreneurship development institute (GEDI) revealed data on the Global Entrepreneurship Index (GEI). In 2018, Bahrain was ranked 35th place, scoring 45.1, which places Bahrain behind Qatar, UAE, and Oman, but better than Kuwait and Saudi Arabia (Table 4).

As innovations play a vital role in a diversified economy as well as contribute to overall socio-economic development. Hence, it is worthwhile to mention a general premise of Bahrain's innovation status and position by using the Global Innovation Index (GII). The GII ranks Bahrain 78th among the 132 economies featured in the GII 2021 (GII, 2021).

Seven (7) pillars measure the Global Innovation Index: *Institutions* (Political environment, regulatory environment, and business environment); *Human capital and research* (education, tertiary education, and research and development (R&D)); *Infrastructure* (information and communication technologies (ICTs), general infrastructure, and ecological sustainability); Market sophistication (credit, investment, trade, diversification, and market scale); *Business sophistication* (knowledge workers, innovation linkages, and knowledge absorption); *Knowledge and technology outputs* (knowledge creation, knowledge impact, and knowledge diffusion); and *Creative outputs* (intangible assets, creative goods and services, and online creativity). The first five pillars make the innovation input sub-index, while the last two make the innovation output sub-index.

In 2020 (Table 5), Bahrain performed less in innovation outputs than innovation inputs. Respectively, it can be observed that innovation inputs are higher compared to 2019 and 2018 while performance of outputs is lower compared to 2019 and 2018. Table 5 indicates that there was a decrease in the GII index (WIPO, 2020).

In the latest report (Table 6), Bahrain's ranks over the last 3 years are with data availability and modifications to the GII model framework influencing year-over-

Table 6 GII rankings for Bahrain (2019–2021)

Year	GII	Innovation inputs	Innovation outputs
2021	78	63	99
2020	79	63	89
2019	78	69	87

Source: World Intellectual Property Organization (WIPO), 2021

year comparisons of the GII rankings. Bahrain's statistical confidence range for the GII 2021 ranking is between ranks 73 and 81.

In sum up, the data showed that in 2021, Bahrain's innovation inputs outperform its innovation outputs. Similarly, Bahrain is ranked 63rd in innovation inputs in 2021, the same as in 2020, but higher than in 2019, while Bahrain is ranked 99th in innovation production. This is a lower ranking than both 2020 and 2019.

2 Business Ecosystem

The business ecosystem implies the entrepreneurship ecosystem (EE) framework, which is crucial in each economy for its smooth development and growth. Global organisations and/or institutes (World Bank—WB, Global Entrepreneurship Monitor—GEM, Global Entrepreneurship and Development Institute—GEDI etc.) are entities that monitor the development of entrepreneurship of a country's ecosystem which turns out to be a good reference for investors. Reports made by these organisations or institutes represent an entrepreneurial outlook that will attract or deter investors worldwide. How robust this ecosystem is, that much will be attractive to investors to pursue a business in a particular country.

The notion of an ecosystem was firstly introduced by Tansley (1935). It was a biological phenomenon where all organisms (both living and non-living) live and interact with each other, which mutually helps them to develop and grow. Moor (1993) defined entrepreneurship ecosystem on the same basis as Tensley (1935) did, but from the business perspective. Moor said that entrepreneurship ecosystem is an interaction whereas all players must interact with each other in the market in order to survive. According to Stem (2018), entrepreneurship ecosystem pillars are formal institutions, entrepreneurship culture, physical infrastructure, demand, networks, leadership, talent, finance, new knowledge, and intermediate service.

Palalić et al. (2020) argued that "The entrepreneurial ecosystem is a very important ingredient in the entrepreneurship development of a country. However, the recipe for how to put those ingredients is crucial. The ecosystem per se alludes in an environment where all players, all kinds of beings and objects live together and somehow support each other in their lives and activities" (p. 25). Thus, the above "recipe" will work if there is a suave interplay between actors in the environment and their mutual collaboration and connectedness. It implies all actors' "symbiotic life" (Dana, 2001) in such an environment. Therefore, the business or entrepreneurship

Table 7 Innovation ranking for GCC countries

No.	GCC member	2019	2020	Change
1	Bahrain	55	79	−24
2	Kuwait	60	78	−18
3	Oman	109	84	+25
4	Qatar	72	70	+2
5	Saudi Arabia	77	66	+9
6	United Arab Emirates	55	34	+21

Source: Global Innovation Index (WIPO). World Intellectual Property Organisation (WIPO) Available at: https://www.wipo.int/edocs/pubdocs/en/wipo_pub_gii_2020.pdf Accessed date: 02.02.2021

ecosystem is "the entrepreneurial ecosystem is a setup of actors like individuals, groups, private and public institutions, and organisations, integrated into legal and cultural outlook, mutually interconnected and whose role influences entrepreneurial activity and gives its positive or negative output in one country" (Palalić et al., 2020, p. 25).

The Kingdom is truly kin to improve the current business environment (business ecosystem). It invests many resources in it as well as in building a strong and developed society through different social and economic activities. One of the pillars of a modern economy is innovation, where Bahrain, in the last 2 years was not fortuned to improve, but the index has been decreased by 24 points (Table 7). It shows that innovation in Bahrain, especially in 2020, has been stopped and streaming down, which indicates that Bahrain was the worst-hit country in terms of innovation. Justification can be found in the recent pandemic (COVID-19) because the primary goal of every government around the globe was to protect the society from it, where lots of resources had to be allocated to fight back against the pandemic.

2.1 Innovation Index: Case of Bahrain

According to WIPO (2020), Bahrain has been ranked at 79th place out of 131 global economies on Global Innovation Index (GII) in 2020 (Table 7).

Regarding Bahrain's business or entrepreneurship ecosystem, it can be said that the main pillars that influence startups or other business opportunities are community, incubators and accelerators, funding, education, corporate partners, and policy and legislation (Bahrain Economic Development Board-BEDB, 2022).[3]

The BEDB (2022) precisely elaborated on these startup pillars and its contribution to society development. In terms of *community*, Bahrain is succeeding in startup

---

[3] Available at: https://www.bahrainedb.com/EDB_AnnualReport_2017/?page=su_six_pillars_of_the_startup_ecosystem, accessed date, 7.4.2022.

projects due to the community's strength and support. The ecosystem benefits from bringing together like-minded entrepreneurs who can share ideas, and business contacts and establish business networks which is seen in a growing number of startup events across Bahrain. *Incubators and accelerators* represent the lifeblood of Bahrain's startups, whereas many established incubators have grown around the country. Local organisations affiliated with Bahrain Development Bank (BDB) like Tamkeen, and Bahrain Business Incubation Centre (BBIC) pushed to the next level the incubators' activities. *Funding* options have always been an essential block in building a great business ecosystem. In the case of Bahrain, this assures that entrepreneurs have abundant financial resources and the best alternative for funding their business and its growth. This could be in the form of a grant, a bank loan, a venture capital investment, an initial public offering, or an angel investor. Tenmou, for instance, is Bahrain's first business angels company that provides initial funding to high-potential innovative Bahraini entrepreneurs.

Furthermore, new crowdfunding regulations have been implemented to enhance the number of possibilities to invest in companies while lowering the cost of obtaining funds. *Education* is crucial, especially regarding profiling entrepreneurs in a business field who are newcomers in the market arena. Therefore, Bahrain pays attention to this important segment in the whole business ecosystem. For example, Bahrain's entrepreneurs enjoy a great pool of various options to develop their competencies and staff skills. The Bahrain Institute for Banking and Finance (BIBF) helps in this by producing world-class training in the Kingdom's fastest-growing sectors, such as new areas of finance through the Bahrain Institute for Banking and Finance (BIBF), or cloud computing through Tamkeen's new AWS certifications.

Moreover, Tamkeen helped 15,000 Bahrainis in training and development programs across various specialisations between 2015 and 2017. The reflection of this training resulted in the job creation of over 1000 employments. Furthermore, Tamkeen is truly kin to provide training programs to foster innovation and help businesses from their inception during the next 3 years (BEDB, 2022). *Corporate partners* are actively engaged in developing a friendly business environment in Bahrain. They act as accelerators, investors, mentors, and sometimes as customers. Corporate partners have provided different perspectives to entrepreneurs and their business aspirations, which enables doing business easy in Bahrain. Finally, the BEDB (2022) argues that all current Laws and Regulations are able to create a synergetic business-friendly environment in one of the world's most cost-effective, profitable, and remunerative markets. Foreign and domestic organisations and companies can function confidently, knowing that the government is committed to assisting them in their business endeavours.

As final thoughts on the business ecosystem, it can be concluded the following:

- The direction of the country, like the Bahrain's vision 2030, helps in establishing, improving, and advancing the business ecosystem. It provides positive results by creating new opportunities and intensifying a diverse economy through entrepreneurship and new startup initiatives. For instance, according to Startup Genome[4] (2022) Bahrain was ideally positioned to play a regionally significant role in developing startup entrepreneurship. It is due to diversified economy; young, educated workforce; and ease of doing business.

- Bahrain is a desirable site for entrepreneurs worldwide since it allows 100% foreign ownership of company assets throughout the economy and has no corporate or income taxes. In recent years, some regional and local accelerators have established themselves as perspective contributors to the business system in the Kingdom of Bahrain. Bahrain has a particularly excellent track record in FinTech, because of its long history as a regional financial centre. Bahrain FinTech Bay (BFB) is a dedicated FinTech cluster that has benefited from the Central Bank of Bahrain's proactive regulatory and institutional backup.
- According to Meero et al. (2020), Bahrain's government and entrepreneur ecosystem partners provide full assistance to Bahrain's entrepreneurs through the *EDB, Tamkeen, Injazz, Bahrain Business Incubator Center*, and other public and private organisations.

As the whole world will depend on global happenings, Bahrain's business landscape will also be contingent on. Nonetheless, the Kingdom will find out other ways to suppress the global impact on doing business in this country.

3 Family Business

Family business is based on a very strong premise, the family, which is regarded in society as the most robust socio-institutional body. The strength and reputation of family businesses vary from one region to another. Different cultural settings put family and family businesses at different societal levels. Some countries like Mexico, North Africa, Middle East, and West Asia are known for being family sensitive, so the family is the first in their lives. In such cultural regions where the family plays a vital role in their lives, family business is also strongly associated with family names. In this context, Ramadani et al. (2020) and Palalić and Smajić (2021) argued that family business is a two-sided entity. One side represents the family and its members while another reflects the family and its members' work and behaviour in society. Meaning, whatever happens in the family influences the family business in the market. Thus, family members must keep their family dynasty crystal clean from any bad reputations and turmoil because such cases can ruin the whole family business. Nonetheless, family and the family business grow in parallel.

Another perspective that keeps family all together is religion. For instance, religion makes people hardworking personalities, and it willingly makes them

---

[4] Available at: https://startupgenome.com/, accessed on 9.4.2022.

contribute to society's development. The Arab World (MENA and GCC) is known as kin for the family's benevolence, strengths, and mutual ties among family members (Hashim et al., 2021). In the Arab world, religion plays the central postulate in raising family members that will, later on, contribute to family development and society and economic development of the nation. Similarly, Dana (2009) discussed religion as the variable that positively influences entrepreneurial activities. Dana noted that the reason is that religions are depositories of values (2009). In this framework, family businesses are also part of this legacy.

Considering the context in which the discussion on family business will be, we argue that family businesses are in an excellent position to change society by providing values to their people. If we look at the revenue, they earn as a family business, it significantly contributes to Bahrain's community. Table 8 shows the top five (5) family businesses from Bahrain listed among 150 family businesses from the Middle East (Family Capital, 2018).

As seen in the Table 8, Bahrain's family businesses are scored so that they are ranked between 48 and 141 place. All five firms have their history and have existed at least for a few decades. Three of them are private, while two of them are public companies. The annual revenue ranges from 300 mils.USD to 1.3 bill.USD. The number of employees is also quite impressive, corresponding from 3500 to 12,526 employees. Different sectors are represented by these companies like banking, construction, distribution, and other industrial conglomerates. All five companies' headquarters are located in the capital city of Manama, the North East region of Bahrain. According to Forbes Middle East (2022), corporates are less influential than family businesses in terms of their contribution to overall GDP value. For instance, family businesses contribute around 60% to the region's GDP and employ 80% of the labour. In terms of monetary value, family business succession was up to $1 trillion in the entire Middle East in the last decade. Most Middle East family businesses are engaged in traditional industries like distribution, franchising, industrials, real estate and construction, and hospitality. However, the recent pandemic negatively affected family businesses' performance, which signalizes that future generations might face similar challenges and yet they could be sadden. Perhaps the pandemic forced family businesses in the Middle East to diversify a lot. For instance, in 2021, out of 100 top family businesses in the Middle East, 87 of them have diversified their business, engaging in different sectors and regions. In terms of gender diversity, however, men's leadership in family business still outperforms women's. Similarly, out of 100 top family businesses only three companies are led by women. However, with generations and a modern approach to leadership, more women could be seen engaged in the family business leadership. Among Middle East countries, Saudi family businesses are more gender diversified. New generations take over, and families modernize. We may see more women in the top roles in the future (Gupta, 2021). It should be noted that family businesses are mainly led by "fathers" of families, while women have taken a minor part in it. However, women's entrepreneurship in Bahrain has grown tremendously (Hashim et al., 2021).

Family businesses in Bahrain are critical drivers in the socio-economic development of the Kingdom. One should be aware that government jobs reached job offer

Table 8 Five (5) of Bahrain's family businesses are listed among the top 150 in the Middle East

Rank	Company	Founded	Family ownership	Public/Private	Country	Headquarters	Revenue in 2018 (in USD$ mil)	Employees	Sector
48	Al Baraka Banking Group	1992	Kamel	Public	Bahrain	Manama	1327.2	12,526	Banks
97	Nass Corporation	1963	Nass	Public	Bahrain	Manama	469.6	6179	Construction
105	Y.K. Almoayyed & Sons	1940	Almoayyed	Private	Bahrain	Manama	577.8	5300	Distributors
130	AMA Group (aka Ahmad Mansoor Al A'Ali)	1940	Al A'Ali	Private	Bahrain	Manama	713.1	4000	Industrial conglomerates
141	Mohammad Jalal & SonsCo WLL	1954	Jalal	Private	Bahrain	Manama	300	3500	Industrial conglomerates

Source: Family Capital (2018)

limits in GCC countries like Bahrain, Oman, and Saudi Arabia. They are into more diversifying industries and businesses, so government jobs will not be any ampler or attractive. Here is where family businesses fill the gap.

Nonetheless, the major contribution to the GDP in Bahrain is from family businesses. According to the argument given by Gomez-Mejia and Herreo (2022); Gomez-Mejia et al. (2007), family businesses are the most common ownership around the globe. Although they differ in size (from micro to large corporations) they still are major contributors to the real GDP in most nations around the world (Ernst et al., 2022). That contribution is over 90% in Bahrain according to unofficial data disseminated via website and magazines' news.

4 Concluding Remarks

As discussed recently by Palalić et al., (2021a); Palalić et al. (2021b) and Dana et al. (2021), Bahrain is in a very important geo-strategic position which provides an excellent opportunity for the country to be exposed, open and close to global business activities. Thus, it becomes a very important hub for investors and business people, giving the Kingdom sufficient basis for various business activities. In the last few decades, such actions have been reflected in various international and bilateral agreements, among which are of great importance, like General Agreement on Tariffs and Trade (GATT) Agreement signed in 1993 and Agreement signed with World Trade Organisation (WTO) Agreement in 1994.

One of the exciting moments, not for Bahrain only but for the whole GCC, is that each GCC member set up a vision for a few decades in the future, which marks such a country being serious in its socio-economic development. Bahrain's vision is set up in 2008 with the name: "The Economic Vision 2030", which was launched by His Majesty King Hamad bin Isa Al Khalifa. This shows the visionary path for the King for Bahrainis to be recognised globally as the ones who initiate good things. In this context, the slogan has been setup "From Regional Pioneer to Global Contender". This vision is supposed to nurture country's sustainability, competitiveness on the global scale, and fairness.

These strategic steps (vision 2020–2030) are crucial in restructuring the country, including the government, society, and business environment (Palalić et al., 2021b). It is hoped that such a momentous strategic vision will positively impact the country in the long term, which will be bounced to domestic human capital as the primary force in socio-economic development of the country. Also, it should be also noted that Bahrain's government has allocated lots of resources via various funds and organisations to complement its vision in reality.

Additionally, Palalić et al. (2021b) noted that Bahrain's government aimed to reduce national poverty and decrease unemployment, especially among youth. In doing this, the government made initiatives in developing other businesses rather than oil and gas production (Dana et al., 2021). The friendly legislation made the country in doing business easy, enabling possibilities of getting various business licenses and a vast pool of skilled and trained labour force. Considering that Bahrain was a nomadic place, it can be said that this country has transformed itself from such an itinerant society into an ultra-modern country (Palalić et al., 2021b; Dana et al., 2021).

Bahrain's business ecosystem is developed in line with the country's vision 2030, where innovation and technology took the place. The Kingdom supports, encourages, and invests in innovation activities and new technology. However, still there are many rooms for improvement. Bahrain is innovation and new technology-oriented because the Kingdom must diversify the economic outlook to be less contingent on oil production. In addition, we are witnessing that all industrialised countries and most developed countries stream toward eco-friendly environmental products (i.e. eco-cars) where petrol will be less consumed. Therefore, one of the imperatives of the Bahrain's economy is to be diversified. However, the antecedent of such diversification is highly innovative industries all over the country. With more patents and/or inventions, the country will have more innovations that will lead to long-term sustainability and a diversified economy.

Although the Global Innovation Index shows low scores (which placed Bahrain behind its neighbours), the real GDP is forecast to grow from 2.6% in 2021 to 4.1% by the end of 2022. This forecasted growth in the real GDP is primarily due to overcoming pandemic effects on the world economy where the consumption of oil has been increased in comparison to the period from 2019 to 2020. However, it is argued that the innovations lead to country's sustainability and thus Bahrain has a lot more to work on. Simply, the Kingdom should create an environment with high innovation index so that the increase in the country's current account does not depend on oil production, but rather on innovation premises. Therefore, the innovation for the country should be imperative and priority number one.

Family businesses' contribution around the world is tremendous and yet different. For instance, that percentage in the United States (US) is 80% than in some other countries (Bahrain Magazine, 2022). Across the twentieth century, the diffusion of family businesses across European (industrialised) countries was astonishing. Out of all registered companies in Italy was 75–95%, in Spain 70–80%, in the UK 75%, in Sweden more than 90%, in Switzerland 85%, in Low Countries (Benelux states: Belgium, Netherland, and Luxemburg) 80–90%, and in Germany, 80% are family businesses (Colli, 2003, p. 15).

Family business survey conducted in the Middle East by Price Waterhouse Coopers (PWC) 89% of them is expected to have annual growth in 2022. Fifty-eight percent of them are to be expanded in other markets (different regions). And, 42% of them stated that conflicts happen occasionally while 59% could be leaders in future sustainable business practices.

After all important remarks above, it can be concluded that family businesses are a constituent part of the Kingdom's economy with a crucial role in implementing the Kingdom's vision. As far as Bahraini family businesses are concerned, several important points can be highlighted.

Exhibit 5 Logo of the Bahrain Family Business Association (BFBA). Source: BFBA (2022)

Firstly, family businesses in Bahrain are the "backbone" of the economy. They contribute immensely to national GDP growth (over 99%). The development of such companies will grow, and they will be even more advanced soon.

Secondly, family businesses in Bahrain are the reality of the whole business ecosystem, so they contribute to creating a friendly business environment.

Thirdly, one of the facts that makes important pillars in being present in Bahrain's society is that family companies have established the Bahrain Family Business Association (Exhibit 5).[5]

This association is for mutual support and cooperation among family businesses across the country. The association's main objectives are to support all types of family enterprises in the Kingdom. In other words, it assists family businesses in building their organisational structures, regulatory frameworks, and work methods, creating family business management modules, and establishing business contacts with counterparts around the globe. Additionally, the association will provide counseling and arbitration services to its members to overcome issues between business partners, inside and outside the Kingdom etc.

Finally, it can be concluded that family businesses' roles are crucial in the Kingdom. They try to provide better future perspectives for newly established (family) companies, which will be part of the "family business" that will lead the country to future development and prosperity.

References

Bahrain Family Business Association. (2022). Accessed January 31, 2022, from https://arab.org/directory/bahrain-family-business-association/

Colli, A. (2003). *The History of Family Business, 1850–2000*. Cambridge University Press.

Dana, L. P. (2001). Introduction networks, internationalization and policy. *Small Business Economics, 16*(2), 57–62.

---

[5] Available at: https://arab.org/directory/bahrain-family-business-association/, accessed on 06.04.2022.

Dana, L. P. (2009). Religion as an Explanatory Variable for Entrepreneurship. *The International Journal of Entrepreneurship and Innovation, 10*(2), 87–99. https://doi.org/10.5367/000000009788161280

Dana, L. P., Ramadani, V., & Palalić, R. (2021). The Future. In *Entrepreneurship In The Gulf Cooperation Council Region: Evolution And Future Perspectives* (pp. 167–173). World Scientific Publishing Europe Ltd. Printed in Singapore.

Dana, L. P., Salamzadeh, A., Ramadani, V., & Palalić, R. (Eds.). (2022). *Understanding Contexts of Business in Western Asia: Land of Bazaars and High-Tech Booms*. World Scientific.

Ernst, R. A., Gerken, M., Hack, A., & Hulsbeck, M. (2022). Family firms as agents of sustainable development: A normative perspective. *Technological Forecasting and Social Change, 174*. (ahead-of-print).

Family Capital. (2018). Accessed February 1, 2022, from https://www.famcap.com/the-middle-east-150-why-family-businesses-matter-so-much-for-the-region/

Global Innovation Index (GII). (2021). Accessed January 31, 2022, from https://www.wipo.int/global_innovation_index/en/2021/

Gomez-Mejia, L. R., Haynes, K. T., Nunez-Nickel, M., Jacobson, K. J. L., & Moyano-Fuentes, J. (2007). Socioemotional Wealth and Business Risks in Family-Controlled Firms: Evidence from Spanish Olive Oil Mills. *Administrative Science Quarterly, 52*(1), 106–137.

Gomez-Mejia, L. R., & Herreo, I. (2022). Back to square one: The measurement of Socioemotional Wealth (SEW). *Journal of Family Business Strategy*. (ahead-of-print).

Gupta, S. L. (2021). Perceived Motivators and Barriers for Entrepreneurship: An Empirical Study of SMEs in Oman. *The Journal of Asian Finance, Economics and Business, 8*(5), 863–872.

Information & eGovernment Authority (IEGA). (2022). Accessed January 31, 2022, from https://www.iga.gov.bh/en/

Meero, A., Rahiman, H., & Rahman, A. A. A. (2020). The prospects of Bahrain's entrepreneurial ecosystem: an exploratory approach. *Problems and Perspectives in Management, 18*(4), 402–413.

Moore, J. F. (1993). Predators and prey: A new ecology of competition. *Harvard Business Review, 71*(3), 75–83.

Palalić, R., Dana, L. P., & Ramadani, V. (2021a). Introduction. *Entrepreneurship In The Gulf Cooperation Council Region: Evolution And Future Perspectives, 7-23.* https://doi.org/10.1142/9781786348081_0002

Palalić, R., Kahwaji, A. T., Eddin, H. N., & Ridić, O. (2021b). Entrepreneurship in Bahrain. In *Entrepreneurship In The Gulf Cooperation Council Region: Evolution And Future Perspectives* (Vol. 1-6). World Scientific Publishing Europe Ltd. https://doi.org/10.1142/9781786348081_0002. Printed in Singapore.

Palalić, R., Knezović, E., Branković, A., & Bičo, A. (2020). Women Entrepreneurship in Bosnia and Herzegovina. In R. Palalić, E. Knezović, & L.-P. Dana (Eds.), *Women Entrepreneurship in Former Yugoslavia*. Springer.

Palalić, R., & Smajić, H. (2021). Socioemotional wealth (SEW) as the driver of business performance in family businesses in Bosnia and Herzegovina: the mediating role of transformational leadership. *Journal of Family Business Management.*, ahead-of-print(ahead-of-print). https://doi.org/10.1108/JFBM-07-2021-0067

Hashim, S., Naldi, L., & Markowska, M. (2021). "The royal award goes to…": Legitimacy processes for female-led family ventures. *Journal of Family Business Strategy, 12*(3), 100358. https://doi.org/10.1016/j.jfbs.2020.100358

Ramadani, V., Memili, E., Palalić, R., & Chang, E. P. C. (2020). *Entrepreneurial Family Businesses: Innovation, Governance, and Succession*. Springer.

Stem, E. (2018). Measuring entrepreneurial ecosystems. In A. O'Connor, E. Stam, F. Sussan, & D. B. Audretsch (Eds.), *Entrepreneurial ecosystems. Place-based transformations and transitions* (pp. 173–196). Springer.

Tansley, A. G. (1935). The use and abuse of vegetational concepts and terms. *Ecology, 16*(3), 284–307.

Websites

Bahrain Economic Development Board (BEDB). (2022). Accessed Apr 7, 2022, from https://www.bahrainedb.com/EDB_AnnualReport_2017/?page=su_six_pillars_of_the_startup_ecosystem

Family Capital. (2018). Accessed Apr 12, 2022, from https://www.famcap.com/the-middle-east-150-why-family-businesses-matter-so-much-for-the-region/

Forbes Middle East. (2022). Accessed Apr 13, 2022, from https://www.forbesmiddleeast.com/lists/top-100-arab-family-businesses-in-the-middle-east-2021/

Global Entrepreneurship and Development Institute (GEDI). (2018) Accessed Apr 9, 2022, from https://thegedi.org/global-entrepreneurship-and-development-index/

IWA Country Classification. (2021). Accessed Apr 18, 2022, from: chrome-extension://efaidnbmnnnibpcajpcglclefindmkaj/viewer.html?pdfurl=https%3A%2F%2Fiwa-network.org%2Fwp-content%2Fuploads%2F2015%2F12%2F2021-Country-Classification-Update.pdf&clen=66479&chunk=true

Ministry of Finance and National Economy: BAHRAIN ECONOMIC REPORT I Q3 2021. (2022). Accessed Apr 6, 2022, from https://www.mofne.gov.bh/Files/cdoc/CI1951-EN%20BEQ%202021%20Q4.pdf

Startup Genome. (2022). Accessed Apr 9, 2022, from https://startupgenome.com/

Trade Economics. (2022). Accessed Apr 6, 2022, from https://tradingeconomics.com/bahrain/gdp-growth-annual

World Intellectual Property Organisation (WIPO). (2020) Accessed Feb 2, 2022, from https://www.wipo.int/edocs/pubdocs/en/wipo_pub_gii_2020.pdf

World Bank (WB). (2020) Accessed Feb 2, 2022, from https://www.worldbank.org/en/country/gcc/publication/economic-update-october-2020-bahrain

World Intellectual Property Organization (WIPO). (2021). Accessed Apr 6, 2022, from https://www.wipo.int/edocs/pubdocs/en/wipo_pub_gii_2021/bh.pdf

Ramo Palalić is an Assistant Professor at the Management Department, College of Economics and Political Science (EQUIS accredited), Sultan Qaboos University (SQU), Oman. His research is in the area of entrepreneurship, leadership, and management. Dr. Palalić has authored and co-authored many articles in globally recognised journals like *Management Decision, International Journal of Entrepreneurial Behavior & Research, International Entrepreneurship and Management Journal*, and alike. Additionally, he has co-authored/co-edited several books and many book chapters in the field of business and entrepreneurship published with internationally prominent publishers (Springer, Routledge, World Scientific). Moreover, Dr. Palalić is serving as the EiC/Associate editors/editor board member in several well-established international journals. Apart from his research, he was involved in business projects in the areas of entrepreneurial leadership and marketing management, in private and public organisations.

Mohamed Rezaur Razzak is an Assistant Professor of Strategic Management, Entrepreneurship, and Family Business at the College of Economics & Political Science (EQUIS accredited), at Sultan Qaboos University in Oman. He obtained his bachelor's degree in mechanical engineering from the University of Texas at Austin followed by MBA from the Southern Methodist University. He completed his PhD with distinction from the University of Malaya specializing in strategy and family business. Dr. Razzak has over 35 years of experience that include industrial and corporate positions followed by a full-time engagement in academia. At present his research interests are in the areas of family business, digital entrepreneurship, emerging business models in the Industry 4.0 era, and sustainable manufacturing and supply chain practices through digitalisation.

Said Al Riyami is an Assistant Professor and the Head of the Department of Management at the College of Economics & Political Science (EQUIS accredited), Sultan Qaboos University, Oman.

Before joining academia, he worked in different public institutions. Dr. Said obtained his PhD and MBA from the University of Texas at El Paso, USA. He has published a number of articles in Web of Science and Scopus Indexed journals. His main research interests include organisational leadership, job embeddedness, organisational behaviour, and proactivity.

Léo-Paul Dana is a Professor at Dalhousie University and Visiting Professor at Kingston University. He is also associated with the Chaire ETI at Sorbonne Business School. A graduate of McGill University and HEC-Montreal, he has served as Marie Curie Fellow at Princeton University and Visiting Professor at INSEAD. He has published extensively in a variety of journals including *Entrepreneurship: Theory & Practice, International Business Review, International Small Business Journal, Journal of Business Research, Journal of Small Business Management, Journal of World Business, Small Business Economics,* and *Technological Forecasting & Social Change.*

Veland Ramadani is a Professor of Entrepreneurship and Family Business at the Faculty of Business and Economics, South-East European University, North Macedonia. His research interests include entrepreneurship, small business management, and family businesses. He authored or co-authored around 180 research articles and book chapters, 12 textbooks, and 22 edited books. He has published in *Journal of Business Research, International Entrepreneurship and Management Journal, International Journal of Entrepreneurial Behavior and Research,* and *Technological Forecasting and Social Change,* among others. Dr. Ramadani has recently published the co-authored book *Entrepreneurial Family Business* (Springer). Dr. Ramadani is co-Editor-in-Chief of *Journal of Enterprising Communities* (JEC). He has received the Award for Excellence 2016—Outstanding Paper by Emerald Group Publishing. In addition, Dr. Ramadani was invited as a keynote speaker at several international conferences and as a guest lecturer by President University, Indonesia, and Telkom University, Indonesia. During 2017–2021, he served as a member of the Supervisory Board of Development Bank of North Macedonia, where for 10 months acted as Chief Operating Officer (COO), as well. In 2021, in a study conducted by Stanford University (USA), he was ranked among the Top 2% of the most influential scientists in the world.

Family Business in Kuwait

Veland Ramadani, Vladimir Dzenopoljac, Mohammad Zainal, and Aleksandra Dzenopoljac

Abstract The current chapter discusses important characteristics of the family business in Kuwait by looking into the links between entrepreneurship, small and medium-sized enterprises, family businesses, and their growth over the years. The authors start by giving a general overview of Kuwait's business ecosystem, which served as a predominant external factor for the development of successful family businesses. One of the key factors in family business development in Kuwait was the country's economic growth after the oil discovery. This growth drove many family businesses. Besides this, the tribal and family linkages were identified as an important driving force. Lastly, the chapter identifies the most successful family businesses in Kuwait and tries to assert the major common characteristics of these companies.

1 Introduction

There is a clear conceptual and logical link between the concept of entrepreneurship and family business. To a certain extent, entrepreneurial companies often tend to become family-owned businesses at a later stage (Poza, 2013). In fact, the

V. Ramadani (✉)
Faculty of Business and Economics, South East European University, Tetovo, North Macedonia
e-mail: v.ramadani@seeu.edu.mk

V. Dzenopoljac
College of Business and Economics, United Arab Emirates University, Al Ain, UAE
e-mail: vdzenopoljac@uaeu.ac.ae

M. Zainal
College of Business Administration, Kuwait University, Sabah Al Salem University City, Kuwait City, Kuwait
e-mail: mohammad.zainal@ku.edu.kw

A. Dzenopoljac
Kragujevac, Serbia

© The Author(s), under exclusive license to Springer Nature Switzerland AG 2023
V. Ramadani et al. (eds.), *Family Business in Gulf Cooperation Council Countries*, Contributions to Management Science,
https://doi.org/10.1007/978-3-031-17262-5_3

researchers in the field of entrepreneurship initially focused on revealing who an entrepreneur is, in terms of his/her characteristics, and what an entrepreneur needs to start and successfully run the business. On the other hand, the research in the field of a family business is more oriented towards explaining what is happening after the business is set up and trying to explain the circumstances surrounding the ending of an entrepreneur's working life. The researchers are exceptionally interested in family business succession issues, like transferring the leadership and ownership to the next generation of family members (Dyer & Handler, 1994). The inception of research in areas of entrepreneurship and family business shows a relatively similar path. The researchers first focused on prescriptive approaches towards the topics in both areas. For example, entrepreneurship research originally started with authors who focused on entrepreneur's role in economic growth and innovative activities (Schumpeter, 1934). Afterwards, the approach was mainly prescriptive, where researchers offered evaluations and suggestions on improving entrepreneurial processes (Hornaday, 1982).

During the early 1970s, the entrepreneurship research re-focused on teaching entrepreneurship and providing consultancy to small businesses. In the field of the family business, the starting point was similar since the researchers were mainly oriented towards providing insights and advice to family business owners on how to improve their performance. This prescriptive focus is almost identical to the entrepreneurship one at the early beginning of the research. Finally, both types of researchers later shifted their attention towards family businesses' role in the economic development of a country and its importance in eliminating unemployment (Brockhaus Sr, 1994). Besides the overlap in thematic inception, the content of entrepreneurship and family business fields are interconnected and possess four distinct intersections. Firstly, the entrepreneurial features are observed and embraced within the family. Secondly, the family members often support entrepreneurial endeavours by assisting the entrepreneur with start-up capital, access to markets, sources of supply, technology, and new ideas. Thirdly, entrepreneurs employ family members, which determines the internal dynamics of the venture. Finally, the intersecting point between entrepreneurship and family business regards the business succession and ownership (Dyer & Handler, 1994).

This early research suffered from providing a clearer understanding of how family business differs from non-family ones in terms of their goals, strategies, and implementation approaches. The research was mainly shifting between prescriptive and descriptive approaches but without a clear connection to strategic aspects of it (Sharma, Chrisman, & Chua, 1997). When assessing the development of the family business topic, it is interesting to note that, in some highly reputed journals (e.g. *Journal of Family Business Management*), the main topics are the description of various family business practices. Additionally, some researchers point out that the primary geographic areas of research include Europe and North America, with growing interest from South America, Oceania, and Asia (Ratten, Fakhar Manesh, Pellegrini, & Dabic, 2021). This confirms the importance of having more practical studies into family business issues in the Middle East. More importantly, the current literature seldom analyses specific country cases in the area of the family business.

Finally, this research only gains its importance once realized that family businesses account for 80% of global business structures and generate jobs for a significant portion of the world population, substantially increasing national revenues (Gagné, Marwick, Brun de Pontet, & Wrosch, 2021).

2 Business Ecosystem

The first recorded inhabitants of one of the islands on Kuwait's coast date back to the fourth century BC. During that time, the ancient Macedonians occupied Failaka Island near the shore of today's Kuwait. In terms of the existence of the state itself, the earliest recorded history reaches back to 1613, when the central Arabian tribes reached the area of Kuwait. These tribes were moving away from a drought that hit their original habitat. The development of Kuwait's economy started soon when the country became a trade hub for various spices between Europe and India. The focus of the trade business in the eighteenth century turned to selling pearls. During this period, the people of Kuwait chose their first emir, Sabah I bin Jaber. The first emir of Kuwait is the ancestor of the Al-Sabah family that rules Kuwait nowadays. This period was when Kuwait grew into the trade and commerce centre in the region, which was also family run. This was mainly due to its convenient location, which successfully linked India, Africa, and Mesopotamia.

Additionally, during this historical period, Kuwait developed one of the largest nautical fleets and managed to create a growing industry and trade of pearls (Dženopoljac, Gerguri-Rashiti, Ramadani, & Dana, 2022). Throughout the eighteenth century, Kuwait traded mainly pearls, spices, dates, horses, and wood (Khedr, 2019). The bazaar played an important role in the trade activities in Kuwait. According to Dana, Etemad, and Wright (2013), the bazaar is a "social and cultural system, a way of life and a general mode of commercial activity, which has been in existence for millennia. In the bazaar, economic transactions are not the focus of activities; instead, the focus is on relationships and alliances. In this scenario, consumers do not necessarily seek the lowest price or the best quality. An individual buys from a friend, sometimes to help the friend and sometimes to ensure that the friend will reciprocate" (p. 113).

A turning point in Kuwait's economic history was the discovery of oil in the 1930s. At that time, the government decided to establish its internationally recognized and accepted borders to keep this newly discovered wealth. At that time, the Ottoman Empire was losing its power after World War I, and they were expelled from Kuwait by the British and Indian armies. The British officially proclaimed Kuwait as being under their protection. The treaty of British protection of Kuwait lasted until 1961. Kuwait became a politically and economically independent country on 19 June 1961. At this time, the Kuwaiti dinar was introduced as an official Kuwait currency and replaced the Gulf rupee that was used until that point (Khedr, 2019).

Exhibit 1 Stock Exchange Building in Kuwait City. Photo ©Veland Ramadani

The oil discovery naturally attracted foreign direct investments (FDI) to Kuwait. Fuelled by the influx of FDI, Kuwait's petroleum industry grew rapidly and made Kuwait one of the wealthiest countries in the region. The economic growth continued, and by 1952, Kuwait had become the most significant oil producer and exporter in the Gulf region. However, the growth was not without its problems. For example, at this time, Kuwait had a dispute with Saudi Arabia about the border and ownership of certain oil fields. This was resolved by a mutual agreement to share the oil reserves in the areas in question. An important milestone in Kuwait's economic development was the taking over of the Kuwait Oil Company by the government of Kuwait during the 1970s. This marked the end of the previous partnership with companies like British Petroleum and Gulf Oil (Khedr, 2019).

Kuwait's economic growth created significant investment and business opportunities in the country. In terms of investment opportunities, this economic growth gave birth to the first unofficial stock exchange in 1978, besides the official market Boursa that was established in 1977 (Exhibit 1). The stock market was referred to as Souk al-Manakh. On this stock exchange, the main objects of trading were shares of companies that resided outside Kuwait, which were not regulated by the Kuwaiti authorities. Most of the trade was made with stocks of companies originating from Bahrain and the United Arab Emirates (Colombo, 2006).

The Souk market was allowed to operate because the Kuwait authorities saw it as a place that could bring about economic innovation. Since Kuwait's official stock market, Boursa, and banking sector were heavily regulated, it was believed that this type of control would limit innovations. However, due to its unregulated nature, inflated expectations fuelled by the economic growth of the country, and oil prices at the time, the market quickly turned to less secure means of trading. Since the market lacked traditional banking and stock market controls, the traders began using post-dated checks as a trading tool (Craig, 2019). This practice was one of the main reasons for the stock's crash in 1982. "In September 1982, the financial authority ordered all debts incurred on trades in the Souk al-Manakh to be turned over to it so regulators could sort the debts out; in doing so, they determined the number of worthless obligations totalled $93 billion (in 1982 US dollars), an amount equivalent to $90,000 (US) for every Kuwaiti—woman, man, or child. By comparison, the annual per capita American income at that time was about $14,000" (Craig, 2019, p. 2).

Besides economic growth, the business ecosystem in Kuwait is shaped by many other important factors. As pointed out by Welsh and Raven (2006), establishing and managing a business, particularly in the retail sector, in the Middle East, and Kuwait in particular is strongly influenced by factors like religion, family, nationality, and culture. For example, religion is sometimes seen as a determining factor in management styles. Some Islamic sects tend to apply more consultative managerial methods, while others see an authoritarian approach as more adequate. The family ties, seen as the consequence of an older tribal system, also affect the businesses. Most of the businesses in the Middle East are owned and run by members of the same family. Certain family traditions, like respect for the elderly, stressing the father's role in the family, and authoritarian management style are affecting how businesses are run in Kuwait. For example, family members are expected to hold important positions within the organizational structure.

On the other hand, there is a tendency to have more non-Kuwaitis in lower managerial positions, especially within smaller companies (Altuhaih & Van Fleet, 1978; Welsh & Raven, 2006). In terms of nationality, in Kuwait predominant workforce in the service sector is composed of non-Kuwaitis. These expatriates usually come from other countries in the Middle East, East Asian countries, and other places. The country is trying to reduce its dependence on expat workers through a Kuwaitization initiative, but this process is slow. In Kuwait, an important factor when doing business is the culture, which leans towards respecting authority and being less limited by behaviours that promote critical thinking and individuality (Welsh & Raven, 2006).

3 Family Business

3.1 Macroeconomic Conditions for Family Business Development

Kuwait is one of the wealthiest countries in the world. According to the 2019 and 2020 data obtained from International Monetary Fund (IMF) and World Bank Data, Kuwait is the 59th country in the world regarding nominal GDP, with a GDP of 134,761 million USD. Regarding GDP per capita, Kuwait ranks as the 40th country in the world with 22,252 USD per capita (Figs. 1 and 2). The Kuwaiti economy heavily depends on exporting petroleum products, and its main partners in this regard are South Korea, China, Japan, India, Singapore, and the United States. On the other hand, the economy of Kuwait is not solely oil dependent. The country has strong production of agricultural fertilisers and other petrochemical products. Additionally, financial services represent an important and growing economy sector, while keeping the tradition of pearl diving. On the import side, the economy of Kuwait imports a major portion of the food products from around the world, together with clothes and technological equipment.

The economy of Kuwait is liberal when assessed against the countries in the region. One of the priorities of Kuwait's government is diversifying into sectors like trade and tourism. The current status of Kuwait's oil reserves is that the country owns around 102 billion barrels (Szczepanski, 2021). Becoming aware of the need to diversify its economy, the government of Kuwait introduced the National Fund for SME Development, with the main objectives of creating jobs for Kuwaitis in the private sector, increasing the participation of small and medium-sized enterprises (SMEs) in the economy, and helping in the creation of a business-friendly

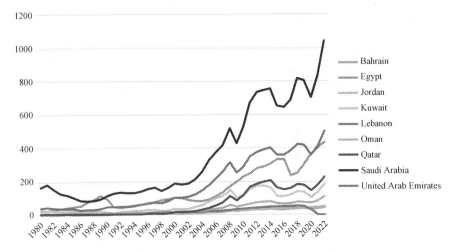

Fig. 1 Kuwait GDP, current prices, billions USD, 1980–2022 (International Monetary Fund)

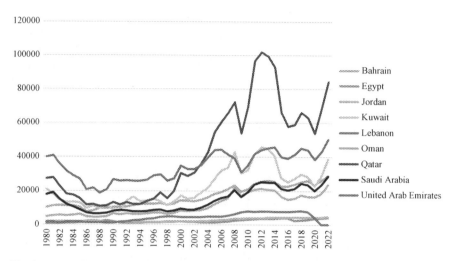

Fig. 2 Kuwait GDP per capita, current prices in USD in 2022, compared to the economies in the region (International Monetary Fund)

environment for SMEs.[1] In Kuwait, 90% of all registered private entities are classified as SMEs. According to the National Fund for SME Development, SMEs are categorised according to their number of employees, assets, and revenues. Companies with less than 50 employees, less than 500,000 KWD in assets, and with achieved revenues below 1,five million KWD falls under the category of an SME. Although SMEs make up 90% of all registered companies, the effective contribution to the GDP is around 3%, with the gross value added by the SMEs of 1216 million KWD in 2019.

In comparison, the share of SMEs' contribution to GDP is around 40% in emerging economies, 50% in high-income economies, and 53% in UAE. Regarding the industry that SMEs in Kuwait belong to, 40% of them are in wholesale/retail trade, together with hotels and restaurants. On the other hand, 33% of SMEs operate in the construction and industry sectors (Dženopoljac et al., 2022).

However, not all SMEs are family-owned businesses, nor all family businesses are SMEs. The difference lies regarding the business development stage and ownership. Family businesses can start as entrepreneurial ventures and grow to become large companies. Some family businesses (e.g. "mom-and-pop-stores") can stay locked into one development stage and remain under the SME category. When viewing ownership, not all SMEs are run and managed by family members. For example, in a family business, the owners (usually a small group of people consisting of family members) have the authority over company decision-making. They can hire and fire CEOs, change the structure and the number of the board of directors, reshape the business and corporate strategies, sell the company, and the

---

[1] The National Fund for Small and Medium Enterprise Development, retrieved from https://nationalfund.gov.kw/en/about-us/vision-and-mission/, accessed on 05 May 2022

like (Baron & Lachenauer, 2021). The characteristics of family businesses largely depend on geographical location, historical impacts, culture, and religion. To be classified as a family business, a particular business should possess the following characteristics: (1) the ownership (at least 15% of the company) needs to be held by two or more members of a family; (2) there should be an evident strategic influence of family members on the management of the firm, either through participating in managing the business, creating the company culture, serving as an advisor, board member, or an active shareholder; (3) to exhibit concern for family relationships; and (4) desire to continue operating through several generations (Poza, 2013, p. 6).

3.2 Distinctiveness of Family Business in the Middle East

To illustrate the significance of family businesses in the region of Middle East, a report prepared by PwC in 2019 revealed that family businesses contribute 60% to the region's GDP and employ around 80% of the workforce. Additionally, the family businesses had passed $1 trillion from one generation of family members to the next. However, these businesses were heavily affected by the COVID-19 pandemic since most of these businesses in the Middle East still operate mainly in traditional industries, like distribution, franchising, industrials, real estate and construction, and hospitality. On the other hand, the negative impact was significantly mitigated because the majority of large family businesses are diversified conglomerates. For example, out of the top 100 family firms in the region, 87% of them are highly diversified (Forbes, 2021a). According to the PwC's Middle East Family Business Survey 2021, one of the key to family businesses' survival during the crisis was diversification, but also business transformation, family values, trust, and constructive conflict, together with focusing the business activities on making a significant impact on the society (PwC, 2021).

During the COVID-19 pandemic, as expected, the family businesses in the Middle East suffered substantial losses. On the other hand, these losses were, to a certain extent, buffered through family businesses' use of conglomerate diversification strategies. It is important to note that the use of conglomerate diversification strategies, as already mentioned, is not a simple response to the ongoing crisis but rather a long-term orientation of most bug family businesses in the region. In order to illustrate the effects of the pandemic on large family conglomerates in the Middle East, PwC's survey from 2021 offers valuable insights (Figs. 3 and 4).

Before the global pandemic, large family businesses in the Middle East showed higher performance than their global counterparts. On the other hand, these businesses were also more challenged during the crisis caused by the drop in oil prices and, soon afterward, the COVID-19 pandemic. Before the COVID-19 pandemic outbreak, family businesses steadily rose from their low points reached in 2018. The pandemic affected the region negatively, which was confirmed by 56% of managers in family businesses, who stated that COVID-19 negatively impacted their sales, whereas 46% of their peers globally confirmed the same (PwC, 2021).

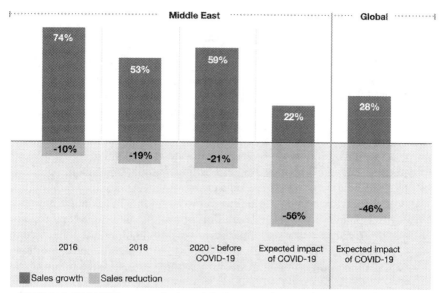

Note: Sums don't total 100, because results show only the percentage of responses indicating sales growth or decline. The range of possible answers to the multiple-choice questions includes 'stable' and 'don't know'.

Fig. 3 Impact of COVID-19 on growth (PwC, 2021, p. 4)

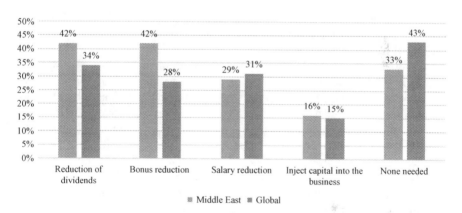

Fig. 4 Sacrifices made by family shareholders (PwC, 2021, p. 4)

One of the key characteristics of family businesses is the ability to adapt to changes quickly. However, this holds true predominantly for smaller companies. In the Middle East, the big family businesses showed this characteristic during the pandemic. In fact, in the region, the families displayed a clear willingness to sacrifice their own gains to keep their businesses running during the global crisis. This is clearly shown in Fig. 4, where the expressed sacrifices by the family businesses in the Middle East were higher compared to their global peers (PwC, 2021).

A very important view of the family businesses in the Middle East was given in the survey performed by PwC (2019), in which four essential pillars of the growth of family businesses were clearly identified. The first one includes *setting the right foundation for the business*. This pillar is dependent on having the right skills and capabilities in an organization from the beginning (66% in the mentioned survey agreed), on quality succession planning (53% of respondents confirmed), and the professionalisation of the businesses (44% agreed). The second pillar of future growth is the need to *create a sustainable business*. This pillar was underpinned by the need to balance between the economic and environmental impact of the business (asserted by 78% of the respondents) and to adequately handle the domestic competition (47% agreeing participants). The third identified pillar was *innovation and digitalization*, in which the key challenges were the very need to innovate (63% of respondents confirmed) and digitalization (44% agreed). The final pillar was the characteristics of the *existing ecosystem*. The two main challenges in this area were coping with existing regulations (63% of respondents confirmed) and the prices of energy and raw materials (44% agreed) (PwC, 2019, p. 5). All these challenges directly affect the nature and future growth of family businesses in Kuwait.

3.3 Distinctiveness of Family Business in Kuwait

The origins of the family business in the Gulf region, or the Gulf Cooperation Council (GCC), which includes Bahrain, Kuwait, Oman, Qatar, Saudi Arabia, and the United Arab Emirates (Beidas-Strom et al., 2011), stems from the tribal nature of the countries' origins. All these specifics regarding the inception of Kuwait as a country and the tribal nature of the region point to the family characteristics of the economy. The primary, family-oriented, approach towards running a business has remained to this day, especially in Kuwait. The tribal societies are founded on the base of family and see it as their cornerstone. This is one of the main reasons why families in this region are an important determining factor in politics and business. For example, the current ruling family in Kuwait is the Al-Sabah family, which has been in power since the eighteenth century, which clearly points to the desire to maintain tradition and stability. Furthermore, the importance of family is also seen in the business area, where 98% of all commercial activities in the GCC region are family run (Welsh & Raven, 2006). In comparison, among the S & P 500 companies in the United States, around 30% comprise family businesses (Zellweger, Kellermanns, Chrisman, & Chua, 2012). Furthermore, the global impact of family firms is substantial, especially knowing that they are estimated to contribute around 70% of worldwide gross domestic product (De Massis, Chirico, Kotlar, & Naldi, 2014).

However, despite its importance, statistical data on family businesses is either sparse or not reliable in Kuwait (Sonfield & Lussier, 2009) and other countries in the region, which is why the main sources of quantitative information about family businesses can be obtained mainly from the third-party analysts, consulting and few government agencies that mainly address entrepreneurship and SMEs sector. Despite this, the field of family business has been increasingly researched in the literature in recent years (Samara, 2021). According to Koch (2011), there is an assumption that more than 30,000 SMEs are registered in Kuwait. They represent around 90% of all registered business entities in the country. Out of this number, approximately 85% are owned by families and individuals. Although the number of SMEs might appear high, the concentration of SMEs is low, amounting to one SME per 43 nationals. For comparison, in Saudi Arabia, there are 25 nationals on one SME. Regarding the sectors, 40% of these companies belong to hotels and restaurants, 30% of the firms operate within construction and utilities, and the rest are within finance, industry, and services (Koch, 2011, p. 4).

Overall, family businesses are an important segment of Kuwait's economy. One of the earliest sectors in which Kuwaiti family firms were involved was trading, initiated initially by being an important port. Later, family businesses entered all important and growing sectors. One of the most important distinguishing characteristics of a family-owned business in Kuwait is its ownership. In the ownership structure, it is prevalent that the elderly members of the family possess almost absolute control and influence the entire decision-making process. Related to the ownership, another important characteristic of many successful family firms is the concentration of the ownership within the family. This allows the company to be more oriented towards long-term success and not seek only short-term profitability. Furthermore, this has worked to these businesses' advantage, since the long-term orientation and financial stability helped them overcome the crises caused by the fluctuations in oil prices in recent years. Another important characteristic of family firms in Kuwait is that most of them were formed several decades ago and at this point, many are widely diversified and transformed into conglomerates. Finally, many of these companies possess a large number of international franchises and have expanded regionally and globally (Kuwait Family Business, 2020).

Related to family businesses is the topic of entrepreneurial venture. An interesting research study on the differences between male and female entrepreneurs by Alowaihan (2004), who identified several important characteristics of Kuwaitis who decide to start their own business. The research showed that Kuwaiti entrepreneurs were well educated, having more than 12 years of education. Additionally, in most cases, the male entrepreneurs started their business before 40 years of age (68% percent of surveyed participants), while in the case of female entrepreneurs, 53% of them started their business before reaching the mentioned age. An interesting fact was also that majority of entrepreneurs in the sample were married, both men and women, 76% and 72%, respectively. In addition, the majority of women (61%) and men (52%) had more than three children. Most women-owned businesses (44%) and men-owned businesses (47%, respectively) were in the service or retail and trade sectors, whereas only 17 percent of men-owned businesses were in the service sector (Alowaihan, 2004, p. 74).

3.4 Success Stories

The last segment depicting the nature and main characteristics of the family business in Kuwait will include a description of the most successful family business in this country. For this purpose, two online sources will be used. The first one is the list of 100 most successful companies in the Middle East, published by Forbes (2021b), where the family companies from Kuwait will be identified. This listed companies from the Middle East stock exchanges that were ranked according to their market value, sales, assets, and profits in 2021. In brief, the total sales of these 100 companies in 2021 reached $550 billion, with an overall net income of $91 billion. Compared to 2020, there is a noticeable drop of 17.9% and 38.5%, respectively.

Additionally, the revenues had also declined as compared to the 2020 list for 57% of the companies, with 67% showing a decrease in net income (Forbes, 2021b). Of the top 100 companies in the Middle East, seven are from Kuwait, namely Kuwait Finance House, Zain Group, Agility, Gulf Bank, The Kuwait Projects Company (KIPCO) Group, Commercial Bank of Kuwait, and Al Ahli Bank of Kuwait. Neither of these companies can be categorised as a family business, according to the earlier criteria established by Poza (2013).

Secondly, we will use the list of top 100 Arab family businesses in the Middle East, also compiled and published by Forbes (2021a). The idea is to identify the most successful companies from Kuwait and see their regional positioning. Interesting findings from the list of top family businesses in the Arab world are that most of these firms are still run by men (women are in the leading positions only in three companies), while 32% of the leading individuals are the founders of the business. In this list, Saudi Arabian companies are mostly present (36 out of 100), while the United Arab Emirates is second (25 out of 100) and Kuwait in the third place with seven companies being on the list (Forbes, 2021a), which is a drop compared to the 2020 list for example when 10 Kuwait companies entered this list (Omran, 2020). The biggest family-owned businesses on this list are:

- Alghanim Industries (ranked 13)
- Alshaya Group (ranked 17)
- Morad Yousuf Behbehani Group (ranked 18)
- Al Sayer Holding (ranked 49)
- Bukhamseen Holding (ranked 59)
- Al Mulla Group (ranked 65)
- BoodaiCorp (ranked 81)

Alghanim Industries was established in 1932 by Yusuf Alghanim, who was the founder of several other big companies in Kuwait, like the Commercial Bank of Kuwait, the Kuwait National Petroleum Company, and the Kuwait Pipes Company. This company is the largest family-owned firm in Kuwait, owning more than 30 businesses in 40 countries. The company is highly diversified and operates in the automotive, engineering, food and beverage, industrial, consumer, and services sectors. The Alghanim family now owns 32.75% of shares in the Gulf Bank, with a market value of $713 million as of April 2021. The current chairman of Alghanim Industries is Kutayba Alghanim who was recognised in December 2020 by the Kuwait Red Crescent Society for his charity work during the COVID-19 pandemic (Forbes, 2021a).

Alshaya Group is a retail company that was founded in 1890 in Kuwait. The company started trading in 1890. It entered a franchise agreement with Mothercare in 1983 in Kuwait. Alshaya continued operating through a franchising system, and today it has 70 different brands across the Middle East and North Africa (MENA) region, Russian Federation, Turkey, and Europe. The company's main area is retail, but it has been diversifying by investing in 34.1% of shares in Mabanee, Kuwait's largest listed real estate company, with an estimated market value of $912 million in April 2021. Alshaya Group has 2800 stores and cafes, employing more than 44,000 people. An exciting endeavour of the company is signing an agreement with Disney in December 2020, obtaining the exclusive rights to open a Disney store in the Middle East (Forbes, 2021a).

Morad Yousuf Behbehani Group is the 18th biggest family-run business in the Middle East. The company was established in 1935 and, like Alghanim Industries, is a diversified conglomerate involved in trading luxury watches, jewellery, luggage, travel accessories, surveying systems, audio-visual equipment, medical equipment, air-conditioning equipment, and telecommunications equipment. The company had a vital role in Kuwait's development because it is responsible for introducing some crucial technologies to Kuwait, like air-conditioning, radio, and TV broadcasting, among others. Regarding financial diversification, the group, owns 5.4% of Gulf Bank and 37.9% of Ahli Bank of Kuwait, with an estimated combined market value of $534 million (Forbes, 2021a).

In 1954, Al-Sayer Holding was founded in Kuwait as a company in the sector of foodstuffs. The business's inception was originally in the 1930s, before the oil discovery. However, the crucial milestone for the company was in automotive trading when they imported the first Toyota Land Cruiser to the Arab world. Additionally, the holding was the world's second official representative of Toyota. Nowadays, Al-Sayer Holding is a diversified corporation operating in sectors like the automotive industry to 18 other industries, including transportation, industrial equipment, financing, investment, real estate, and others. Al-Sayer invested 10% of Warba Bank in Kuwait, estimated at $124 million in April 2021 (Forbes, 2021a).

Ranked as the 59th largest family business in the Arab world, Bukhamseen Holding is a conglomerate that operates in industries like trade, real estate, construction, finance and banking, hospitality, industrial production, and media, among others. Like the previous family businesses from Kuwait, Bukhamseen is well invested in the banking sector. The company co-founded the Kuwait International Bank and has 35.8% of shares in this bank. Other stock investments include listed firms, like Al-Arabiya Real Estate Company, Egyptian Gulf Bank, and Qatar First Bank. The company also entered the insurance sector by investing in Warba Insurance Company, one of Kuwait's oldest insurance companies. Finally, the company possesses a financial asset managing company, Arab Investment Company, which manages assets worth $1 billion (Forbes, 2021a).

Al Mulla Group is another example of a long-lasting, successful, family-owned company from Kuwait. The company was founded in 1938 by Mr. Abdullah Saleh Al Mulla. The group operates in sectors like automotive, engineering, financial services, rental and leasing, trading, and manufacturing. Additionally, the company has a rental and leasing subsidiary with over 9000 vehicles and 22 branches in Kuwait. The group owns 40 subsidiaries representing more than 200 internationally recognised brands. The group's distinctive brands in Kuwait are Chrysler, Fiat, Dodge, Mitsubishi Motors, and Daimler AG Mercedes-Benz. The company is ranked as the 65th largest family business in the Arab world and employs more than 15,000 people worldwide.

The last Kuwait-based family-owned company is BoodaiCorp, which was established in 1954. The current chairman is Jassim Boodai. The company is active in media, building materials, commodities, engineering, heavy machinery, logistics, print media, public transport, publishing and distribution, travel, and aviation sectors. The company is the owner of Alrai TV, which is a privately-owned satellite TV channel in Kuwait. Apart from this, BoodaiCorp owns City Bus, a privately-owned public transport service that operates with a fleet of 552 vehicles. BoodaiCorp owns more than 54% of Jazeera Airways, over 84% in the Alrai Media Group Company, and around 95% of Hilal Cement Company. These companies are listed on Kuwait Stock Exchange (Forbes, 2021a).

Each of the presented family businesses had humble beginnings, and some of them were established before the oil discovery in the 1930s (e.g. Al Sayer Holding, Alshaya Group). The discovery of oil accelerated their growth and initiated forming of many other family firms. These family businesses have several common characteristics. Firstly, all these companies are still run and managed by family members, who are all men. Secondly, these family businesses are highly diversified. Some of them originally started in one industry (e.g. Al-Sayer), but later entered several other attractive sectors at the time. In addition, some of these companies further diversified their assets by investing in successful listed corporations in Kuwait. This leads to the third common characteristic of described companies, which is leaning towards investing in financial sector, predominantly banks. The fourth commonality among the largest Kuwaiti family businesses is their longevity. All these corporations exhibit a long, uninterrupted, and successful business history, with clear and consistent roles of family members as the chairpersons. Finally, all these corporations embarked on their journey around the time when Kuwait saw its biggest economic expansion, which was around the time the oil was discovered. These conglomerates were directly or indirectly connected to developing country's infrastructure, trade, and importing important technologies and goods. This was mainly driven by the rise of the standard of living, which further opened the doors to family businesses that operated in the fields of imports and retail. Nowadays, this success cannot be seen among the family businesses in Kuwait. Immensely few small family businesses can grow among these existing giants. The main growth possibilities in Kuwait are coming through new technologies, more franchise agreements, and important construction projects. However, small businesses cannot hope to get any of the big contracts due to the lack of resources, on one side, and intense competition from the powerful family-run businesses.

4 Concluding Remarks

The current chapter focused on describing and analysing the context for family business development in Kuwait. The used approach here is deductive in nature, which includes moving from the general areas towards the particular areas. This is used when starting from a theory, testing the hypotheses, and having feedback by revising the starting theory (Locke, 2007; Woiceshyn & Daellenbach, 2018). The business ecosystem was analysed in the first instance, where the specificities of Kuwait's economic history and development were portrayed. The key event in this regard was the discovery of oil in the 1930s and becoming an independent country in 1961. The oil discovery was a key driver of economic development. Today, the country belongs to the group of high-income countries and possesses 10% of the world's oil reserves, making it the fourth biggest per capita income in the world, and second in the GCC region, after Qatar. Kuwait's economy is described as petroleum based, in which 50% of the GDP and 90% of the government income comes from the sale of oil. In terms of entrepreneurship and small business, there is an increase in registered start-ups. In Kuwait, SMEs contribute to GDP by around 3%, which is considered low when compared to the 50% that is the world average (Abdullah, 2021).

Investment opportunities arose as a result of Kuwait's rapid economic development, primarily in the construction and commerce industries. Since Kuwait was described as a tribal society whose influence can be seen in the business sphere, the majority of Kuwaiti families are large, with six to twelve close relatives making up the majority (Al-Thakeb, 1985). In Kuwait, powerful tribes and families have long exerted their authority. To benefit from the country's growing economy, families with a greater emphasis on entrepreneurialism launched construction and import businesses that received significant government contracts. To open a business in Kuwait, the government's official website states that the following conditions must be met: There must be at least two people involved in the business, and all partners must be free of criminal convictions and have valid residency visas. The non-Kuwaiti partner's share cannot exceed 49 percent, and he or she must show proof that he or she paid his or her share of the capital. A limited liability company cannot be formed between a husband and wife (Kuwait Government Online, 2021). Family businesses in Kuwait have flourished and are now major players in the market thanks to a third factor.

Besides economic growth, the business ecosystem in Kuwait is shaped by many other important factors. As pointed out by Welsh and Raven (2006), establishing and managing a business, particularly in the retail sector, in the Middle East, and Kuwait in particular, is strongly influenced by factors like religion, family, nationality, and culture. In Kuwait, not all SMEs are family owned, nor are all family businesses

SMEs. The difference lies in business development stage and ownership. Family businesses can start as entrepreneurial ventures and grow to become large companies. Some family businesses can stay locked into one development stage and remain under the SME category. When viewing ownership, not all SMEs are run and managed by family members. For example, in a family business, the owners (usually a small group of people consisting of family members) have the authority over company decision-making.

Family businesses are an important part of Kuwait's economy. In the early stages of economic development, Kuwaiti family firms were mainly involved in trading, but later, these businesses entered all important and growing sectors. When discussing the ownership structure, it is very common in Kuwait family firms that the elderly members possess almost absolute control and influence the entire decision-making process. Related to the ownership, another important characteristic of many successful family firms is the concentration of the ownership within the original or nuclear family. This allows the company to be more oriented towards long-term success and not to seek only short-term profitability. This has proven efficient and effective since the long-term orientation and financial stability helped them to overcome various crises caused by the fluctuations in oil prices and the COVID-19 pandemic in recent years. Another important characteristic of family firms in Kuwait is that majority of them were formed several decades ago, and at this point, many of them are widely diversified and transformed into conglomerates. Finally, many of these companies possess many international franchises and have expanded regionally and globally (*Kuwait Family Business*, 2020).

The chapter emphasized several highly prominent companies by using the Forbes' list of top 100 family businesses in the Middle East (Forbes, 2021a). Seven family-owned companies from Kuwait entered this list, namely Alghanim Industries, Alshaya Group, Morad Yousuf Behbehani Group, Al-Sayer Holding, Bukhamseen Holding, Al Mulla Group, and BoodaiCorp. These most successful Kuwaiti companies exhibit several common characteristics. Firstly, all these companies are still run and managed by family members, who are all men. Secondly, these family businesses are highly diversified. The third common characteristic of described companies is their leaning toward investing in the financial sector, predominantly banks. The fourth commonality is their longevity. All these corporations exhibit a long, uninterrupted, and successful business history, with clear and consistent roles of family members as the chairpersons. Finally, all these corporations embarked on their journey around the time when Kuwait saw its most significant economic expansion, which was around the time the oil was discovered. These conglomerates were directly or indirectly connected to developing country's infrastructure, trade, and importing of important technologies and goods.

References

Abdullah, N. M. (2021). Family entrepreneurship and banking support in Kuwait: Conventional vs Islamic banks. *Journal of Family Business Management, 11*(3), 313–331. https://doi.org/10.1108/JFBM-06-2020-0049

Al-Thakeb, F. T. (1985). The Arab family and modernity: Evidence from Kuwait. *Current Anthropology, 26*(5), 575–580.

Alowaihan, A. K. (2004). Gender and business performance of Kuwait small firms: A comparative approach. *International Journal of Commerce and Management, 14*(3/4), 69–82. https://doi.org/10.1108/10569210480000185

Altuhaih, S., & Van Fleet, D. (1978). Kuwait management: A study of selected aspects. *Management International Review, 18*(1), 13–22.

Baron, J., & Lachenauer, R. (2021). *Harvard business review family business handbook: How to build and sustain a successful, enduring enterprise*. Harvard Business Press.

Beidas-Strom, S., Rasmussen, T. N., Robinson, D. O., Charap, J., Cherif, A., Khamis, M. Y., et al. (2011). *Gulf cooperation council countries (GCC): Enhancing economic outcomes in an uncertain global economy*. IMF.

Brockhaus, R. H., Sr. (1994). Entrepreneurship and family business research: Comparisons, critique, and lessons. *Entrepreneurship Theory and Practice, 19*(1), 25–38.

Colombo, J. (2006). Kuwait's Souk al-Manakh Stock Bubble. *The Bubble Bubble*. Retrieved on July 3, 2022 from http://www.thebubblebubble.com/souk-al-manakh/

Craig, B. R. (2019). The Souk al-Manakh Crash. *Economic Commentary*. Retrieved on July 3, 2022 from https://www.clevelandfed.org/newsroom-and-events/publications/economic-commentary/2019-economic-commentaries/ec-201920-kuwait-souk-al-manakh.aspx

Dana, L. P., Etemad, H., & Wright, R. W. (2013). Toward a paradigm of symbiotic entrepreneurship. *International Journal of Entrepreneurship and Small Business, 5*(2), 109–126.

De Massis, A., Chirico, F., Kotlar, J., & Naldi, L. (2014). The temporal evolution of proactiveness in family firms: The horizontal S-curve hypothesis. *Family Business Review, 27*(1), 35–50.

Dyer, W. G., & Handler, W. (1994). Entrepreneurship and family business: Exploring the connections. *Entrepreneurship Theory and Practice, 19*(1), 71–83. https://doi.org/10.1177/104225879401900105

Dženopoljac, V., Gerguri-Rashiti, S., Ramadani, V., & Dana, L.-P. (2022). The context for business in Kuwait. In L.-P. Dana, A. Salamzadeh, V. Ramadani, & R. Palalić (Eds.), *Understanding contexts of business in Western Asia* (pp. 259–275). World Scientific Publishing Company.

Forbes. (2021a). *Top 100 Arab family businesses in the Middle East*. Retrieved on July 3, 2022 from https://www.forbesmiddleeast.com/lists/top-100-arab-family-businesses-in-the-middle-east-2021/

Forbes. (2021b). *Top 100 companies in the Middle East*. Retrieved on July 3, 2022 from https://www.forbesmiddleeast.com/lists/top-100-companies-in-the-middle-east-2021/

Gagné, M., Marwick, C., Brun de Pontet, S., & Wrosch, C. (2021). Family business succession: What's motivation got to do with it? *Family Business Review, 34*(2), 154–167.

Hornaday, J. A. (1982). Research about living entrepreneurs. In J. A. Hornaday (Ed.), *Encyclopedia of entrepreneurship* (pp. 20–34). Prentice-Hall.

Khedr, A. A. (2019). *Kuwait legal system and research*. Retrieved on July 3, 2022 from https://www.nyulawglobal.org/globalex/Kuwait1.html

Koch, E. (2011). *Challenges to SME Development in Kuwait*. UNDP.

Kuwait Family Business. (2020). Retrieved on July 3, 2022 from https://www.researchandmarkets.com/reports/5263856/kuwait-family-business?utm_source=dynamic&utm_medium=BW&utm_code=rjvk9r&utm_campaign=1394607+-+Kuwait+Family+Business+Report+2020+-+Private+Equity+Partnership+a+Preparatory+Step+to+Public+Listing&utm_exec=cari18bwd

Kuwait Government Online (2021). *Establishing a new company*. Retrieved on July 3, 2022 from https://e.gov.kw/sites/kgoenglish/Pages/Services/MOCI/EstablishmentNewCompany.aspx

Locke, E. A. (2007). The case for inductive theory building. *Journal of Management, 33*(6), 867–890.

Omran, H. (2020). *10 Kuwaiti companies among top 100 Arab family businesses in the Middle East 2020. Leaders.* Retrieved on July 3, 2022 from https://www.forbesmiddleeast.com/leadership/leaders/10-kuwaiti-companies-among-top-100-arab-family-businesses-in-the-middle-east-2020

Poza, E. J. (2013). *Family business* (third ed.). Cengage Learning.

PwC. (2019). *Future-proofing Middle East family businesses–Achieving sustainable growth during disruptive times.* Retrieved on July 3, 2022 from https://www.pwc.com/m1/en/publications/documents/family-business-survey-2019.pdf

PwC. (2021). *Diversifying, investing and digitising–Family businesses are transforming for a sustainable future.* Retrieved on July 3, 2022 from https://www.pwc.com/m1/en/publications/family-business-survey/2021/documents/middle-east-family-business-survey-2021.pdf

Ratten, V., Fakhar Manesh, M., Pellegrini, M. M., & Dabic, M. (2021). The journal of family business management: A bibliometric analysis. *Journal of Family Business Management, 11*(2), 137–160. https://doi.org/10.1108/JFBM-02-2020-0013

Samara, G. (2021). Family businesses in the Arab Middle East: What do we know and where should we go? *Journal of Family Business Strategy, 12*(3), 100359. https://doi.org/10.1016/j.jfbs.2020.100359

Schumpeter, J. A. O. R. (1934). *The theory of economic development; an inquiry into profits, capital, credit, interest, and the business cycle.* Harvard University Press.

Sharma, P., Chrisman, J. J., & Chua, J. H. (1997). Strategic management of the family business: Past research and future challenges. *Family Business Review, 10*(1), 1–35.

Sonfield, M. C., & Lussier, R. N. (2009). Non-family-members in the family business management team: A multinational investigation. *International Entrepreneurship and Management Journal, 5*(4), 395–415. https://doi.org/10.1007/s11365-009-0109-4

Szczepanski, K. (2021). *Kuwait: Facts and history.* Retrieved on July 3, 2022 from https://www.thoughtco.com/kuwait-facts-and-history-195060

Welsh, D. H. B., & Raven, P. (2006). Family business in the Middle East: An exploratory study of retail management in Kuwait and Lebanon. *Family Business Review, 19*(1), 29–48. https://doi.org/10.1111/j.1741-6248.2006.00058.x

Woiceshyn, J., & Daellenbach, U. (2018). Evaluating inductive vs deductive research in management studies. *Qualitative Research in Organizations and Management: An International Journal, 13*(2), 183–195. https://doi.org/10.1108/QROM-06-2017-1538

Zellweger, T. M., Kellermanns, F. W., Chrisman, J. J., & Chua, J. H. (2012). Family control and family firm valuation by family CEOs: The importance of intentions for transgenerational control. *Organization Science, 23*(3), 851–868.

Veland Ramadani is a Professor of Entrepreneurship and Family Business at the Faculty of Business and Economics, South-East European University, North Macedonia. His research interests include entrepreneurship, small business management, and family businesses. He authored or co-authored around 180 research articles and book chapters, 12 textbooks, and 22 edited books. He has published in the *Journal of Business Research, International Entrepreneurship and Management Journal, International Journal of Entrepreneurial Behavior and Research*, and *Technological Forecasting and Social Change*, among others. Dr. Ramadani has recently published the co-authored book Entrepreneurial Family Business (Springer). Dr. Ramadani is co-Editor-in-Chief of the *Journal of Enterprising Communities* (JEC). He has received the Award for Excellence 2016—Outstanding Paper by Emerald Group Publishing. In addition, Dr. Ramadani was invited as a keynote speaker at several international conferences and as a guest lecturer by President University, Indonesia, and Telkom University, Indonesia. During 2017–2021, he served as a member of the Supervisory Board of Development Bank of North Macedonia, where for 10 months acted as Chief Operating Officer (COO), as well. In 2021, in a study conducted by Stanford University (USA), he was ranked among the Top 2% of the most influential scientists in the world.

Vladimir Dzenopoljac is the Associate Professor of Strategic Management at the College of Business and Economics within the United Arab Emirates University, UAE. Previously, he was the Associate Professor and the Director of the MBA programme at the College of Business Administration, American University of the Middle East, Kuwait. Vladimir's academic career started at the Faculty of Economics, University of Kragujevac, Serbia, where he worked for 13 years. At the same university, he received his PhD degree in the field of intellectual capital and value creation. He is an active researcher and published a significant number of journal articles in the areas of intellectual capital, knowledge management, strategic management, and entrepreneurship. Alongside his academic career, Vladimir provided business consultancy services in the areas of strategy development and execution, business planning, and financial planning and analysis.

Mohammad Zainal is a Professor of Applied Statistics at the College of Business Administration, Kuwait University, teaching Business Statistics and Computer Courses. He is also the current Dean of the College, and the Chair of the Board of Trustees at the Center of Excellence in Management. Mohammad's research interests include Parametric Estimation in the Skew-Symmetric Distributions, Optimization in High Dimensions, Goodness-of-Fit and Nonparametric Estimation, and the Application of Computer Methodologies to facilitate "Real-World" Solutions to Complex Business problems. Also, his research involves providing Applied Problem-Solving in Operations Strategies in SMEs and Innovation Orientation and Performance of Family Businesses. He has published in the *Journal of Family Business Management, Journal of Enterprising Communities: People and Places in the Global Economy, Frontiers in Immunology, Sustainability 2022, Periodicals of Engineering and Natural Sciences*, and the *International Journal of Business and Globalisation*.

Aleksandra Dzenopoljac is an independent researcher and industry practitioner with extensive corporate experience in areas like marketing, human resource management, strategic and business planning, as well as in the field of supply chain management. Aleksandra received her bachelor's and master's degrees from the University of Kragujevac, Serbia, in the field of Marketing. In the last 15 years, she has been occupying junior and senior managerial positions in companies in the logistics, manufacturing, and entertainment industries. She is a PhD candidate and publishes in the fields of intellectual capital and entrepreneurship.

Family Business in Qatar

Aidin Salamzadeh and Léo-Paul Dana

Abstract Family businesses are an integral part of most Gulf Cooperation Council countries. As leading families of these countries dominate the public, private, and third sectors, it is crystal clear that they will lead most socio-economic activities. Qatar is a leading country in terms of managing public and private sectors by families. Thus, it is essential to have a clear insight into its situation. Therefore, this chapter investigates the general business ecosystem of the country and then further discusses the dominant families and family businesses in Qatar. It also provides more details about the dynamics of Qatari family businesses, and the chapter concludes with some remarks for policymakers and practitioners. Besides, it suggests some directions for future research about family businesses in Qatar.

1 Introduction

Not many emerging economies have reached the peak in business cycles, while Qatar has been among the leading economies in terms of growth and development. Qatar has always struggled to realise sustainable development goals while creating wealth like other major oil and gas exporting countries (Zain & Kassim, 2012). Despite all the positive characteristics of the country, its growing population coupled with a decreased level of natural resources and mismanagement experiences have led to a set of problems for its economy (Kabbani & Mimoune, 2020). Qatari officials have extensively planned to harness the negative impacts of the "resource curse" and "Dutch disease". Generally, such prosperous countries focus on creating value

---

A. Salamzadeh (✉)
Faculty of Management, University of Tehran, Tehran, Iran
e-mail: salamzadeh@ut.ac.ir

L.-P. Dana
Rowe School of Business, Dalhousie University, Halifax, NS, Canada
e-mail: lp762359@dal.ca

Exhibit 1 The Pearl-Qatar (Source: https://pixabay.com/images/id-3850752). *Note:* Free for commercial use; No attribution required

through investing the oil and gas income in diversified sectors (Welsh & Raven, 2006; Ogidi, 2013).

Thus, Qatari entrepreneurs have designed and produced many innovative and entrepreneurial products that have changed the country's business environment and relevant structures. This fact can be a double-edged sword in various countries. On the one end of the continuum, countries like Qatar, Australia, and Norway have done their best to succeed and create wealth for their nation. On the other end, countries such as Iraq, Zimbabwe, and Libya have suffered from mismanaging their natural resources (Salamzadeh et al., 2013; Tajpour et al., 2020; Islam et al., 2022). It is noteworthy that, back in the 1970s, the Gulf Cooperation Council (GCC) countries initiated such constructive movements and took advantage of their oil and gas income to improve their socio-economic indexes (Guerrero et al., 2014, 2015; Rochmaedah & Suseno, 2022). The Pearl-Qatar, which is an artificial island, is a symbol of such movements (Exhibit 1).

The country's geopolitical position is of paramount importance, as the Persian Gulf mainly surrounds it, and Qatar is a neighbour to Iran, Saudi Arabia, Bahrain, and the UAE. Its area is almost 11,571 km^2. Qatar gained its independence in 1971, following several oil and gas discoveries and exploitations in the 1960s. Like Bahrain, Qatar's business environment was mainly focused on pearling and fishing before those discoveries (Balaguer, 2016; Palalić et al., 2022). Doha is the densest city and the capital of Qatar. The population is less than three million, according to the latest census. Interestingly, more than 75% of the population are men. Only almost 12% are the local population, and around 88% are immigrants. These made the business environment unique (Shaaban, 2016; Deshingkar et al., 2019).

As a tribal monarchy that is ruled by various tribes, especially the Al-Thani family, the structure of the family business is well contextualised in Qatar. The government centrally manages the oil and gas resources, which has helped them provide a better taxation regime, citizenship services, and high-quality health and educational systems. Then, family businesses are an integral part of the business environment (Costa & Pita, 2020; Al-Khatib & Al-Abdulla, 2001). As reported by Forbes in 2021, five Qatari enterprises were listed among "Forbes' top 100 Arab family businesses".[1] Such a culture could facilitate the operations of the family firms and lead to their success (Miroshnychenko & De Massis, 2022). Thus, this chapter provides more in-depth insights into Qatar's business ecosystem, then explores the family businesses in the country, and concludes with some remarks on the Qatari family businesses and future directions for researchers.

2 Business Ecosystem

Historically, the business ecosystem of Qatar has experienced a significant turn after the oil and gas discoveries and exploitations. The primary businesses were pearl hunting and fishing for many years (Exhibit 2). The major exploitations in the 1940s transformed the whole economy and provided a fertile ground for business development in the country. The standard of living increased significantly, and relevant policies accelerated the movement (Crystal, 1995). The government does not charge any income tax, and the other tax rates are lower than in most countries worldwide. Moreover, other economic indexes, such as a low unemployment rate, reveal the potential of the state's economy. For many years, the country was listed among the top ten countries in terms of its GDP per capita (Jabeen et al., 2015). Qatari officials take advantage of foreign labour forces from various countries, and therefore, people from different countries with distinct backgrounds and knowledge work in this country. The country was listed as the wealthiest country in the world three times (Awadallah, 2020). Some neighbour countries such as Saudi Arabia and UAE have imposed sanctions against Qatar, but those sanctions did not affect the country's economic growth to a great extent. Table 1 summarises the primary indicators of the country (Dana et al., 2021; Ratten et al., 2009). As it is shown in the table, Qatar has significantly improved in terms of its socio-economic indicators, especially during the past decade.

A significant part of the economy is composed of the businesses related to *oil and gas* explorations which have turned the country from a poor to one of the wealthiest countries worldwide. The economy experienced a downturn in the 1980s due to low oil prices (Al-Kubaisi, 1984). Thus, Qatar entered into a recession stage for some

---

[1] Al Faisal Holding, AlFardan Group, Almana Group, Abu Issa Holding, and Almuftah Group.

Exhibit 2 A ship is waiting to go fishing (Source: https://pixabay.com/photos/ship-doe-qatar-43 6820/). Note: Free for commercial use; No attribution required

years, but hopefully, the economy recovered in the 1990s. People from various countries immigrated to Qatar accordingly in those years. Based on some projections, the oil fields will be depleted in the next few years, but Qatar still enjoys significant gas reserves for exploration and exploitation. According to the statistics, the country belongs the third-largest gas reserves globally. It is noteworthy that the government reports reveal that offshore oil and gas fields may provide the economy with extra natural resources in the upcoming years. In addition to oil and gas resources, they take advantage of the gas condensate and refined products (Dana et al., 2022).

In addition to the oil and gas industries, Qatari officials and the government have invested extensively in *industrial settings* following a diversification strategy. The oil and gas incomes mainly support these industries, and the industrialisation wave has initiated in the past few decades. The industrial development plans are defined and implemented accordingly. As shown in Table 1, in 2020, industry (including construction) comprises almost 52% of the GDP in terms of the created value added (Exhibit 3). In contrast, exports of goods and services comprised around 48% of the GDP. Besides, construction materials, fertilisers and pharmaceuticals are among the other significant industries in Qatar (Tok et al., 2021).

Qatar is also well-known for its *financial sector* and its key players. Although they experienced severe challenges back in 2008, this section has dramatically grown in the aftermath of the great recession. Qatar's banking and financial institutions followed the footsteps of the leading financial institutions and created many

Family Business in Qatar

Table 1 Country profile

	1990	2000	2010	2020
Population, total (millions)	0.48	0.59	1.86	2.88
Population growth (annual %)	3.1	3.8	11.5	1.7
Surface area (sq. km) (thousands)	11.6	11.6	11.6	11.5
Population density (people per sq. km of land area)	41	51	159.9	250.7
Poverty headcount ratio at national poverty lines (% of the population)	..	..	..	..
Poverty headcount ratio at $1.90 a day (2011 PPP) (% of the population)	..	..	..	..
GNI, Atlas method (current US$) (billions)	..	18.2	118.09	161.3
GNI per capita, Atlas method (current US$)	..	28,400	63,620	55,990
GNI, PPP (current international $) (billions)	..	52.84	219.77	253.73
GNI per capita, PPP (current international $)	..	89,190	118,390	88,070
People				
Income share held by the lowest 20%	..	..	..	..
Life expectancy at birth, total (years)	76	77	79	80
Fertility rate, total (births per woman)	4	3.2	2.1	1.8
Adolescent fertility rate (births per 1000 women aged 15–19)	49	20	13	9
Contraceptive prevalence, any method (% of married women aged 15–49)	32	43	38	..
Births attended by skilled health staff (% of total)	100	100	100	100
Mortality rate, under 5 (per 1000 live births)	21	13	9	6
Prevalence of underweight, weight for age (% of children under 5)	..	..	..	..
Immunisation, measles (% of children aged 12–23 months)	79	91	99	90
Primary completion rate, total (% of relevant age group)	73	94	95	96
School enrollment, primary (% gross)	98.5	105	102.6	103.9
School enrollment, secondary (% gross)	80	91	105	..
School enrollment, primary and secondary (gross), gender parity index (GPI)	1	1	1	..
Prevalence of HIV, total (% of population aged 15–49)	0.1	0.1	0.1	0.1
Environment				
Forest area (sq. km) (thousands)	0	0	0	0
Terrestrial and marine protected areas (% of the total territorial area)	..	..	..	5.8
Annual freshwater withdrawals, total (% of internal resources)	337	333.5	439.4	447.9
Urban population growth (annual %)	3.7	4	11.7	1.8
Energy use (kg of oil equivalent per capita)	13,703	18,432	14,890	..
CO$_2$ emissions (metric tons per capita)	26.33	36.68	33.54	32.42
Electric power consumption (kWh per capita)	9591	14,348	14,209	..
Economy				
GDP (current US$) (billions)	7.36	17.76	125.12	144.41

(continued)

Table 1 (continued)

	1990	2000	2010	2020
GDP growth (annual %)	..	3.9	19.6	−3.6
Inflation, GDP deflator (annual %)	..	−5	7	−15.1
Agriculture, forestry, and fishing, value added (% of GDP)	..	0	0	0
Industry (including construction), value added (% of GDP)	..	..	73	52
Exports of goods and services (% of GDP)	..	67	62	49
Imports of goods and services (% of GDP)	..	22	24	41
Gross capital formation (% of GDP)	..	20	31	44
Revenue, excluding grants (% of GDP)	..	..	..	..
Net lending (+) / net borrowing (−) (% of GDP)	..	..	..	..
States and markets				
Time required to start a business (days)	..	..	11	9
Domestic credit provided by financial sector (% of GDP)	..	..	..	..
Tax revenue (% of GDP)	..	..	..	..
Military expenditure (% of GDP)	10.7	3.9	1.5	..
Mobile cellular subscriptions (per 100 people)	0.8	20.4	117.8	131.8
Individuals using the Internet (% of population)	0	4.9	69	99.7
High-technology exports (% of manufactured exports)	..	..	0	7
Statistical Capacity Score (overall average) (scale 0–100)	..	..	..	..
Global links				
Merchandise trade (% of GDP)	72	84	78	54
Net barter terms of trade index (2000 = 100)	..	100	183	101
External debt stocks, total (DOD, current US$) (millions)	..	..	..	..
Total debt service (% of exports of goods, services, and primary income)	..	..	..	..
Net migration (thousands)	−10	214	605	200
Personal remittances, received (current US$) (millions)	..	..	0	652
Foreign direct investment, net inflows (BoP, current US$) (millions)	5	252	4670	−2434
Net official development assistance received (current US$) (millions)	3	..	..	..

Source: World Development Indicators database, World Bank

success stories at regional and global levels. In addition, they have been experienced in offering Islamic banking and financial services to their clients. Thus, the Islamic finance sector has added so many initiatives to the financial industry, in general, in the past decades. The capital market is also active and has provided the business ecosystem's players with various opportunities. Venture capitalists actively seek investment opportunities in innovative and technological sectors.

Tourism is another primary industry in Qatar. The government and the Qatar Tourism and Exhibitions Authority defined and implemented various plans to increase the number of tourists, which were successful, especially in the last two

Exhibit 3 Skyscrapers in Doha (Source: https://pixabay.com/images/id-3850732). *Note:* Free for commercial use; No attribution required

decades. They spent billions of dollars to establish new touristic platforms such as hotels, recreation centres, and amusement parks. Infrastructures such as the Hamad International Airport were part of these plans (Theodoropoulou & Alos, 2020). The government focused on cultural tourism to expand the sector and empower the local communities and businesses (Exhibit 4).

Moreover, the *transportation industry* developed exponentially as the population grew during the past decades. Besides, the need for more reliable transportation solutions was highlighted. They invested significantly in roads, railways, airports, marine transportation facilities, and related vehicles and infrastructures. This sector includes both national and international solutions to help the country's continuous socio-economic development (Shaaban & Maher, 2020; Shaaban & Adalbi, 2021).

Then, the general business ecosystem of the country includes oil and gas, industrial, financial, tourism, and transportation sectors. It is noteworthy that the *creative industries* and the startup ecosystem have evolved extensively during the last decade (Kebaili et al., 2015; Salamzadeh, 2018). The Qatar Venture Investment reports, which are published annually, show the existing trends and achievements, including the key stakeholders, the venture investment impact, the evolutionary path of the fundings, the general investment landscape, and the ecosystem map. The interactions between these sectors and the creative industries have changed the shape of doing business in Qatar (Almoli, 2018; Moayedfar & Chafi, 2019; Nawaz & Koç, 2020).

Exhibit 4 Tourism in Qatar (Source: https://pixabay.com/images/id-6977918). *Note:* Free for commercial use; No attribution required

3 Family Business

As mentioned earlier, Qatar, like many other Arab countries in this region, comprises various tribes, clans, and well-known families (Kamrava, 2017). Thus, many leading companies are family businesses in nature. This characteristic is somehow unique and makes the economy not comparable to the rest of the world—except for the Arab world (Al-Balam & Raza, 2009). Family interactions with the government could change many written and unwritten rules of the game and doing business (Ennis, 2015). These businesses contribute significantly to the socio-economic development of the country. Based on some estimations, they create around 60% of the GDP, and more than 80% of the labour force work in these firms. These estimations reveal the importance of these firms (Ramadani et al., 2018). However, the coronavirus pandemic has recently affected many of these firms (Kawamorita et al., 2020; Hameed et al., 2021; Pereira et al., 2021; Salamzadeh & Dana, 2021). It is not much unexpected to witness that most of these companies are managed by male C-level managers and shareholders, while females are marginalised. According to some recent studies, issues such as balancing the business and family expectations, preparing a succession plan, clarifying the corporate governance style, and lack of some soft and hard skills to manage family firms could impact the success or failure of any typical family business in Qatar.

The dynamics of family businesses and their interactions are critical to the general socio-economic development of the country. These dynamics might act as a double-edged sword. While some positive interactions might lead to joint venture agreements, mutual funds, and collaborations, the negative ones might lead to unfair

Table 2 Qatari tribes and family origins

	Purported origins	Families and clans
Ajamis	Persian	Al-Ansari, Al-Fardan, Al-Emadi, Mustafawi
Huwala	Original Sunni Arabs who moved from the Arabian shore to Persia and came back between the 1930s and 1950s	Al-Ansari, Al Darwish, Al Fakhroo, Al-Hammadi, Al Jaber, Al Jaidah, Al-Malki, Al Muftah, Al Jassim, Al Ahmed
Arab tribes	Qatari tribes tracing their origins to the Arabian Peninsula	Al Thani, Al Attiya, Al Bin Ali, Al Buainain*, Al-Humaidi, Al-Kaabi, Al Khater, Al-Kubaisi, Al-Kuwari, Al-Maadeed, Al-Malki, Al-Jahni, Al-Marri, Al-Mohannadi*, Al Mahmood, Al Mana, Al-Mannai, Al Misned*, Al-Muraikhi, Al-Noaimi, Al-Sulaiti*, Al-Suwaidi

Source: Kamrava (2017)

competition. Thus, family connections and interactions are vital factors in this business ecosystem. In his seminal work, Kamrava (2017) categorised the families and tribes, which could help us better understand the Qatari society. It is worth mentioning that the starred ones (*) are originally from Bahrain, and Bahraini families were originally Persian. The Table 2 shows the low number of families and tribes. It, in turn, highlights the importance of considering families and tribes as critical institutions (rules of the game).

Besides, Kamrava (2017) enlists the major families and their family firms. These families manage large-scale family businesses that are, in fact, "corporates" with various companies. He has further discussed the ties between families and their interactions. They have histories of collaborations and competitions, some of which are mentioned in Kemrava's (2017) paper. These families are categorised into two major groups:

(i) *Arab tribes*: Al Attiyah [Al Attiya Group (with nine subsidiaries)], Al Faisal (Al Thani) [Al Faisal Holding], Al-Kaabi [Al-Kaabi Contracting & Trading Co.], Al-Kuwari [Al-Kuwari Group], Al Mana [Al-Mana Group (with 13 subsidiaries)], Al-Mannai [Al-Mannai Group (with 29 subsidies)], and Al Misnad [Al Misnad Group].

(ii) *Ajamis or Huwala*: Al-Fardan [Al-Fardan Group], Al Haidar [Sulaiman Al Haj Haider and Sons Co.], Al Jaidah [Jaidah Group (with eight subsidiaries) Jaidah Brothers], Al-Khouri [Taleb Group], Al Muftah [Almuftah Group (with 33 subsidiaries)], and Mustafawi [Al Mustafawi Trading & Engineering].

These family firms, which have already benefited from the previous economic booms, contribute to Qatar's economy. Nevertheless, as the power is concentrated in these families, if some unexpected or sudden crisis happens, the economy might be affected by such incidents. Incidents such as conflicts while running businesses or transitions between different generations of the families could significantly affect the economy. Besides, the lack of defining sound institutional structures could lead to instabilities in these businesses, and therefore, these family businesses might be significantly affected. Some of these family businesses have experienced relevant challenges which affected their profitability and stability.

Qatari family businesses have shown great interest in improving the entrepreneurial talents of their members and those interested in joining their firms. They insist on increasing the loyalty level of their members and the family members through various ceremonies and considering initiatives. Besides, they believe in creating long-term strategic relationships to commit to their members and partners. Qatari family firms stick to their ethical standards and traditions while considering the generally accepted social and commercial values and respecting social responsibilities. The elder members of family firms contribute to transferring their entrepreneurial skills and success factors to the next generations who will manage the firms after them (Salamzadeh et al., 2014; Ramadani et al., 2015, 2017; Toska et al., 2021).

Although family firms have been studied extensively in the literature (Dana & Ramadani, 2015; Tajpour et al., 2021; Chang et al., 2022), a few studies have explored this phenomenon in Qatar (Faisal, 2011; Rabasso et al., 2015). Nevertheless, the findings have revealed that the context matters, and while the questions are the same, the answers are not necessarily similar to the results in the Western contexts. For instance, in Western countries, business succession generally continues until the second generation sells or acquires the company and some of the members or all of them leave the business, while in Qatar, many family businesses have experienced the transition to the third or fourth generations. Also, most family members of the next generations do not leave the company. Another critical point to mention is the presence of women Qatari entrepreneurs in the family businesses, which has changed the competition scene (Faisal, 2013).

4 Concluding Remarks

The family businesses in GCC countries have specific characteristics which make them unique. For instance, due to their Arabic culture, close family relationships and strong family ties, the existence of tribes and clans, and other similar features have created a distinguished context for Qatari family businesses (Hawi et al., 2022). On the one hand, these characteristics highly affect businesses' success or failure. On the other hand, as the number of families is limited, and strong family ties exist in Qatar's business environment, the family business context has become distinguished compared to the rest of the world. Moreover, as family-related issues are culturally entangled with family businesses in Qatar, many cultural and societal factors have affected the business environment. Thus, for instance, friendship or hatred between various family firms directly affects the dynamics of the business ecosystems. In addition, the population diversity and immigrants who work in male-dominant Qatari family firms have added to the complexity of doing business in family businesses. As an integral part of their wealthy nation, Qatari family firms invest in various international and regional projects. Interestingly, family businesses in Qatar do business in multiple sectors, including oil and gas, construction, tourism, transportation, and creative sectors of the economy. Also, the public sector is highly dependent on the family ties of a set of families who are the country's governing officials. It has made the situation more complex and somehow more flexible. In sum, this chapter provides insights into the general business environment and the family businesses in Qatar. Future researchers might focus on more detailed aspects of doing business in family firms in Qatar and their challenges. Besides, the role of female family members in those businesses is overlooked, and therefore, future studies could investigate the gender role. Finally, the family firms' ecosystem dynamics might be explored and studied in future studies.

References

Al-Balam, N. M., & Raza, S. A. (2009). Impact of family responsibilities on career success among employees working in the semi-government sector in the state of Qatar. *International Journal of Arab Culture, Management and Sustainable Development, 1*(2), 208–223. https://doi.org/10.1504/IJACMSD.2009.030663

Al-Khatib, F., & Al-Abdulla, M. (2001). The state of Qatar: A financial and legal overview. *Middle East Policy, 8*(3), 110–126. https://doi.org/10.1111/1475-4967.00031

Al-Kubaisi, M. A. M. (1984). *Industrial development in Qatar, 1950–1980: A geographical assessment* (doctoral dissertation, Durham University).

Almoli, A. (2018). *Towards knowledge-based economy; Qatar science and technology park, performance and challenges* (doctoral dissertation, Hamad Bin Khalifa University (Qatar)).

Awadallah, E. (2020). Measuring the effectiveness of selected corporate governance practices and their implications for audit quality: Evidence from Qatar. *Afro-Asian Journal of Finance and Accounting, 10*(1), 24–47.

Balaguer, P. A. (2016). Linking education and business across geography of erasmus+ improving relationships between vocational training and job market. *Journal of Entrepreneurship, Business and Economics, 4*(1), 73–84.

Chang, E. P., Zare, S., & Ramadani, V. (2022). How a larger family business is different from a non-family one? *Journal of Business Research, 139*, 292–302. https://doi.org/10.1016/j.jbusres.2021.09.060

Costa, J., & Pita, M. (2020). Appraising entrepreneurship in Qatar under a gender perspective. *International Journal of Gender and Entrepreneurship, 12*(3), 233–251. https://doi.org/10.1108/IJGE-10-2019-0146

Crystal, J. (1995). *Oil and politics in the Gulf: Rulers and merchants in Kuwait and Qatar* (Vol. No. 24). Cambridge University Press.

Dana, L. P., & Ramadani, V. (2015). *Family businesses in transition economies*. Springer International Publishing.

Dana, L. P., Palalic, R., & Ramadani, V. (Eds.). (2021). *Entrepreneurship in the Gulf cooperation council region: Evolution and future perspectives*. World Scientific.

Dana, L. P., Salamzadeh, A., Ramadani, V., Palalić, R., & (Eds.). (2022). *Understanding contexts of business in Western Asia: Land of Bazaars and High-Tech Booms*. World Scientific Publishing.

Deshingkar, P., Abrar, C. R., Sultana, M. T., Haque, K. N. H., & Reza, M. S. (2019). Producing ideal Bangladeshi migrants for precarious construction work in Qatar. *Journal of Ethnic and Migration Studies, 45*(14), 2723–2738. https://doi.org/10.1002/bse.2222

Ennis, C. A. (2015). Between trend and necessity: Top-down entrepreneurship promotion in Oman and Qatar. *The Muslim World, 105*(1), 116–138.

Faisal, M. N. (2011, November). Family Businesses in Qatar: A Study of Select Issues. In *Qatar Foundation Annual Research Forum Volume 2011 Issue 1* (Vol. 2011, No. 1, p. AHP11). Hamad bin Khalifa University Press (HBKU Press).

Faisal, M. N. (2013, November). A study of the role of women in family businesses in Qatar. In *Qatar Foundation Annual Research Forum Volume 2013 Issue 1* (Vol. 2013, No. 1, pp. SSHP-032). Hamad bin Khalifa University Press (HBKU Press).

Guerrero, M., Urbano, D., & Salamzadeh, A. (2014). Evolving entrepreneurial universities: Experiences and challenges in the middle eastern context. In *Handbook on the Entrepreneurial University*. Edward Elgar Publishing.

Guerrero, M., Urbano, D., & Salamzadeh, A. (2015). Entrepreneurial transformation in the Middle East: Experiences from Tehran universities. *Technics Technologies Education Management, 10*(4), 533–537.

Hameed, N. S. S., Salamzadeh, Y., Rahim, N. F. A., & Salamzadeh, A. (2021). The impact of business process reengineering on organisational performance during the coronavirus pandemic: Moderating role of strategic thinking. *Foresight*. https://doi.org/10.1108/FS-02-2021-0036

Hawi, A., Al-Kuwari, F., & Garonne, C. (2022). Entrepreneurship development in Qatar. In *Entrepreneurial rise in the Middle East and North Africa: The influence of quadruple helix on technological innovation*. Emerald Publishing Limited.

Islam, A., Maideen, M. B. H., Abd Wahab, S., binti Ya'akub, N. I., & Latif, A. S. A. (2022). Conceptualising the smart holistic growth paradigm for small and medium businesses: An integrative perspective. *Journal of Entrepreneurship, Business and Economics, 10*(1), 212–264.

Jabeen, F., Katsioloudes, M. I., & Das, S. S. (2015). Is family the key? Exploring the motivation and success factors of female Emirati entrepreneurs. *International Journal of Entrepreneurship and Small Business, 25*(4), 375–394.

Kabbani, N., & Mimoune, N. B. (2020). The role of families in supporting youth employment in Qatar. In *Families and Social Change in the Gulf Region* (pp. 96–116). Routledge.

Kamrava, M. (2017). State-business relations and clientelism in Qatar. *Journal of Arabian Studies, 7*(1), 1–27. https://doi.org/10.1080/21534764.2017.1288420

Kawamorita, H., Salamzadeh, A., Demiryurek, K., & Ghajarzadeh, M. (2020). Entrepreneurial universities in times of crisis: Case of COVID-19 pandemic. *Journal of Entrepreneurship, Business and Economics, 8*(1), 77–88.

Kebaili, B., Al-Subyae, S. S., Al-Qahtani, F., & Belkhamza, Z. (2015). An exploratory study of entrepreneurship barriers: The case of Qatar. *World Journal of Entrepreneurship, Management and Sustainable Development, 11*(3), 210–219. https://doi.org/10.1108/WJEMSD-03-2015-0014

Miroshnychenko, I., & De Massis, A. (2022). Sustainability practices of family and nonfamily firms: A worldwide study. *Technological Forecasting and Social Change, 174*, 121079.

Moayedfar, R., & Chafi, M. M. (2019). A theoretical expansion of talent allocation model: Evidence from selected developing countries from 2014-2018. *Entrepreneurial Business and Economics Review, 7*(4), 57–72.

Nawaz, W., & Koç, M. (2020). *Case study: Qatar. In industry, university and government partnerships for the sustainable development of knowledge-based society* (pp. 71–106). Springer.

Ogidi, E. (2013, November). Entrepreneurial Learning in a Multigenerational Family Business: Evidence from Nigeria. In *Qatar Foundation Annual Research Forum Volume 2013 Issue 1* (Vol. 2013, No. 1, pp. SSHSP-03). Hamad bin Khalifa University Press (HBKU Press).

Palalić, R., Dana, L. P., Ramadani, V., & Salamzadeh, A. (2022). The context for business in Qatar. In L. P. Dana, A. Salamzadeh, V. Ramadani, & R. Palalić (Eds.), *Understanding contexts of business in Western Asia: Land of bazaars and high-tech booms*. World Scientific Publishing.

Pereira, J., Braga, V., Correia, A., & Salamzadeh, A. (2021). Unboxing organisational complexity: How does it affect business performance during the COVID-19 pandemic? *Journal of Entrepreneurship and Public Policy, 10*(3), 424–444. https://doi.org/10.1108/JEPP-06-2021-0070

Rabasso, C. A., Briars, M., & Rabasso, J. (2015). Royal family business in Qatar and the emirates through sports club management: "green washing" or a sustainable model? The cases of FC Barcelona and Manchester City. *International Journal of Employment Studies, 23*(2), 5–25.

Ramadani, V., Ademi, L., Ratten, V., Palalić, R., & Krueger, N. (2018). Knowledge creation and relationship marketing in family businesses: A case-study approach. In *Knowledge, learning and innovation* (pp. 123–157). Springer.

Ramadani, V., Fayolle, A., Gërguri-Rashiti, S., & Aliu, E. (2015). The succession issues in family firms: Insights from Macedonia. In *Family businesses in transition economies* (pp. 199–221). Springer.

Ramadani, V., Hisrich, R. D., Anggadwita, G., & Alamanda, D. T. (2017). Gender and succession planning: Opportunities for females to lead Indonesian family businesses. *International Journal of Gender and Entrepreneurship, 9*(3), 229–251. https://doi.org/10.1108/IJGE-02-2017-0012

Ratten, V., Dana, L. P., & Welpe, I. M. (2009). *Drivers of international entrepreneurship in Asia. In handbook of research on Asian entrepreneurship*. Edward Elgar Publishing.

Rochmaedah, D., & Suseno, B. D. (2022). Strategy of former Indonesian migrant workers from Qatar in the era of the Covid-19 outbreak. *International Journal of Business, Management and Economics, 3*(2), 185–195. https://doi.org/10.47747/ijbme.v3i2.699

Salamzadeh, A. (2018). *Start-up boom in an emerging market: A niche market approach. In competitiveness in emerging markets* (pp. 233–243). Springer.

Salamzadeh, A., & Dana, L. P. (2021). The coronavirus (COVID-19) pandemic: Challenges among Iranian startups. *Journal of Small Business & Entrepreneurship, 33*(5), 489–512. https://doi.org/10.1080/08276331.2020.1821158

Salamzadeh, A., Farsi, J. Y., & Salamzadeh, Y. (2013). Entrepreneurial universities in Iran: A system dynamics model. *International Journal of Entrepreneurship and Small Business, 20*(4), 420–445. https://doi.org/10.1504/IJESB.2013.057200

Salamzadeh, Y., Nejati, M., & Salamzadeh, A. (2014). Agility path through work values in knowledge-based organisations: A study of virtual universities. *Innovar, 24*(53), 177–186.

Shaaban, K. (2016, April). Investigating the reasons for choosing a major among the engineering students in Qatar. In *2016 IEEE Global Engineering Education Conference (EDUCON)* (pp. 57–61). IEEE. https://doi.org/10.1109/EDUCON.2016.7474531.

Shaaban, K., & Adalbi, M. A. (2021, July). Smart City transportation system in developing countries: The case of Lusail City, Qatar. In *International Conference on Applied Human Factors and Ergonomics* (pp. 445–452). Springer.

Shaaban, K., & Maher, A. (2020). Using the theory of planned behavior to predict the use of an upcoming public transportation service in Qatar. *Case Studies on Transport Policy, 8*(2), 484–491. https://doi.org/10.1016/j.cstp.2019.11.001

Tajpour, M., Hosseini, E., & Salamzadeh, A. (2020). The effect of innovation components on organisational performance: Case of the governorate of Golestan Province. *International Journal of Public Sector Performance Management, 6*(6), 817–830. https://doi.org/10.1504/IJPSPM.2020.110987

Tajpour, M., Salamzadeh, A., Salamzadeh, Y., & Braga, V. (2021). Investigating social capital, trust and commitment in family business: Case of media firms. *Journal of Family Business Management*. https://doi.org/10.1108/JFBM-02-2021-0013

Theodoropoulou, I., & Alos, J. (2020). Expect amazing! Branding Qatar as a sports tourism destination. *Visual Communication, 19*(1), 13–43. https://doi.org/10.1177/1470357218775005

Tok, E., Koç, M., & D'Alessandro, C. (2021). Entrepreneurship in a transformative and resource-rich state: The case of Qatar. *The Extractive Industries and Society, 8*(2), 100708. https://doi.org/10.1016/j.exis.2020.04.002

Toska, A., Ramadani, V., Dana, L. P., Rexhepi, G., & Zeqiri, J. (2021). Family business successors' motivation and innovation capabilities: The case of Kosovo. *Journal of Family Business Management*. https://doi.org/10.1108/JFBM-11-2021-0136

Welsh, D. H., & Raven, P. (2006). Family business in the Middle East: An exploratory study of retail management in Kuwait and Lebanon. *Family Business Review, 19*(1), 29–48. https://doi.org/10.1111/j.1741-6248.2006.00058.x

Zain, M., & Kassim, N. M. (2012). Strategies of family businesses in a newly globalised developing economy. *Journal of Family Business Management, 2*(2), 147–165. https://doi.org/10.1108/20436231211261880

Aidin Salamzadeh is an assistant professor at the University of Tehran. His interests are startups, new venture creation, and entrepreneurship. Aidin serves as an associate editor in "Revista de Gestão", "Innovation and Management Review" (Emerald), "Entrepreneurial Business and Economics Review", "Journal of Women's Entrepreneurship and Education" as well as an editorial advisory in "The Bottom Line" (Emerald). Besides, he is a reviewer in numerous distinguished international journals. Aidin is a member of the European SPES Forum (Belgium), the Asian Academy of Management (Malaysia), Ondokuz Mayis University (Turkey), and the Institute of Economic Sciences (Serbia). He is the co-founder of the Innovation and Entrepreneurship Research Lab (London).

Léo-Paul Dana is a professor at Dalhousie University. He is also a member of the Entrepreneurship and Innovation Chair, which is part of LabEx Entreprendre at the Universite de Montpellier. A graduate of McGill University and HEC-Montreal, he has served as Marie Curie Fellow at Princeton University and Visiting Professor at INSEAD. He has published extensively in a variety of journals, including *Entrepreneurship: Theory and Practice, International Business Review, International Small Business Journal, Journal of Business Research, Journal of Small Business Management, Journal of World Business, Small Business Economics* and *Technological Forecasting and Social Change*.

Family Business in Oman

Mohammad Rezaur Razzak, Ramo Palalić, and Said Al-Riyami

Abstract Although the overwhelming majority of the privately owned businesses in Oman are family-owned businesses with an overall GDP contribution of over 60%, yet there appears to be a paucity of academic publications that elaborate on the overall scenario of family businesses in Oman. Other than some regional case studies about Omani family firms, there appears to be a dearth of sufficient finer-grained analysis of what makes Omani family businesses unique. Therefore, this study examines the existing academic literature as well as non-academic publications from dependable sources such as reports from international consulting firms, to compile a nuanced analysis of how Omani family-controlled enterprises are different in many ways because of the idiosyncratic cultural context of Oman. The narrative in this chapter begins with an overall introduction of how family firms differ from non-family ones. Particular focus is laid on the theory of socioemotional wealth, the ability and willingness paradox, and family commitment as a source of competitiveness and organisational resilience. Thereafter, an overview about the Sultanate of Oman and the business ecosystem is presented. The subsequent sections elaborate on the idiosyncrasies of Omani family firms along with anecdotal evidence through examples of a few Omani family-controlled business organisations both large and small. Finally, the chapter ends with concluding remarks that relate the previous discourse about family businesses with the context of Omani family businesses.

1 Introduction

Family businesses are not only ubiquitous but are also the most dominant category of business organisations around the world in terms of ownership (Gomez-Mejia & Herreo, 2022). Such organisations range from micro-level businesses to SMEs to large publicly listed companies, and are recognised to be a major contributor to GDP

M. R. Razzak (✉) · R. Palalić · S. Al-Riyami
College of Economics & Political Science, Sultan Qaboos University, Seeb, Oman
e-mail: m.razzak@squ.edu.om; r.palalic@squ.edu.om; saidalriyami@squ.edu.om

© The Author(s), under exclusive license to Springer Nature Switzerland AG 2023
V. Ramadani et al. (eds.), *Family Business in Gulf Cooperation Council Countries*,
Contributions to Management Science,
https://doi.org/10.1007/978-3-031-17262-5_5

growth and new employment generation in most nations (Ernst et al., 2022). Furthermore, Ghouse et al. (2019) reveal that majority of the entrepreneurial ventures are driven by family money (i.e. love capital) and continue to be closely guarded and nurtured by individuals who typically would not have made it thus far without the support of their family. Until an organisation becomes sustainable, the backing of the family through material and psychological resources remains the primary catalyst in the growth of new business organisations (Daspit et al., 2021). As a result, family-owned or family-controlled businesses are distinct in many ways from non-family firms. The extant literature related to factors that basically differentiate the behaviour of family business owners from those that are not considered as family firms, is based on three core ideas. The first idea can be understood through the lens of the *socioemotional wealth theory*, the second is based on the concept of *ability and willingness paradox*, and the last one is the idea of *family commitment* as a source of competitiveness and organisational resilience (De Massis et al., 2018; Gomez-Mejia & Herreo, 2022).

2 The Socioemotional Wealth Theory

The term socioemotional wealth became recognized following a seminal study by Professor Luis R. Gomez-Mejia and colleagues, who examined family-owned olive oil mills in the Cordoba region of Spain (Gomez-Mejia et al., 2007). The study investigated the behaviour of family-firm owners when they were offered economic benefits by the state economic cooperative in exchange for the role of the authorities in the governance of these firms. The findings indicated that majority of the family-owned businesses were reluctant to relinquish any sort of control over their businesses, and were ready to sacrifice any potential economic benefits in order to preserve the family's control over the enterprise. This disposition of family-firm owners to sacrifice economic benefits to preserve their family's control over the businesses is the core premise of the concept of socioemotional wealth. The theory of socioemotional wealth takes the position that family-firm owners prioritize social and emotional goals of the family as much as or even perhaps more than economic goals (Gomez-Mejia et al., 2007). The construct was later operationalized by subsequent researchers such as Berrone et al. (2012), Hauck et al. (2016), and others, to argue that socioemotional wealth is made up of five dimensions, known as FIBER (shown in Fig. 1).

The dimensions of socioemotional wealth (or SEW in short) shown in Fig. 1 are: (i) *family control and influence*, (ii) *identification of the family with the firm*, (iii) *binding social ties of the family*, (iv) *emotional attachment of the family*, and (v) *renewal of family bonds through dynastic succession*. Many of these dimensions appear to be conceptually overlapping yet they are quite distinct (Prugl, 2018).

The first dimension of SEW reflects the desire of the family to preserve control over key decisions in the business, and is unanimously accepted as a distinctive feature of family businesses. The second dimension reflects the sense of pride that a

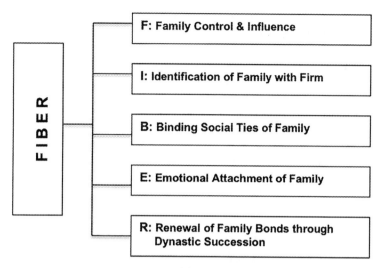

Fig. 1 Dimensions of socioemotional wealth. *Source:* Hauck et al. (2016)

family derives from having the name of the family being associated with the business organisation. This perception creates a sense of identity for the family members in the society they dwell in. The third dimension represents the social bonds that are formed due to the business activities of the family firm with different external and internal stakeholders. Some of these bonds translate into valuable resources that lead to competitive advantages for the firm. For instance, working with a group of suppliers over a long time, in some cases over multiple generations, can create binding social ties that provide the firm with valuable leverage in ensuring sustainable supply of inputs. Similarly, close working relationships with talented non-family employees have shown that family firms have lower employee turnover compared to their non-family counterparts (Tabor et al., 2017). The fourth dimension 'emotional attachment' is about the emotional connections that are developed between the family members because the family business provides close interaction between the members whose livelihoods are interconnected through the business. The last dimension is about the desire for continuity of the family legacy. As a result, the incumbent family business leaders look forward to nurturing their next generation to take over from them at some time and continue the legacy (Gerken et al., 2022).

A major advantage of the SEW approach is that it derives its' evolution from and mirrors a substantial body of peer-reviewed academic research on family businesses (Laffranchini et al., 2018). When contrasted to other paradigms used in family business studies, the other approaches find it difficult to adjust to the context of family-owned enterprises (Swab et al., 2020). Decades of research corroborate with the notion that family business owners are naturally inclined to place great emphasis on their SEW endowment. Although, SEW was originally derived from the behavioural agency model, the SEW model is recognized to be more versatile as a construct, and is well recognized among family business scholars, as evidenced by the increasing number of published articles in top-tier journals as a testament to its' analytical adaptability (Gomez-Mejia & Herreo, 2022).

Unlike other fields of management, the field of family business studies lacks any theory that can be specifically applicable to the realm of family businesses. The development of a homegrown theory of family business is a highly sought-after goal, and family business scholars have recognized that the SEW Model holds promise in paving the path towards such a theoretical development that has been an elusive mirage so far (Ernst et al., 2022). This is mainly because the multidimensional conceptualisation of SEW provides avenues to unravel a common thread that can explain the idiosyncrasies of family firms. The SEW perspective has now emerged as a dominant paradigm that is being looked at with great interest by family firm researchers in their *'Quest for the Holy Grail'* (i.e. Theory of Family Business) (Bringham & Payne, 2019).

There is an intense debate among family business scholars on whether SEW is directly related to a firm's business performance or whether they are independent of each other or whether they are related to each other through other behavioural dimensions such as entrepreneurial orientation of the family, family commitment towards the firm, and governance systems (Gerken et al., 2022). Chrisman and Holt (2016) elaborated on this issue by stating that the relationship between SEW and firm performance is likely mediated by other variables, not considered so far, that reflect collective family behaviour in connection to the firm.

3 Ability and Willingness Paradox

In order to comprehend the features that distinguish family firms from other organisations, the theorem by De Massis et al. (2016) about *'Ability'* and *'Willingness'* presents an interesting rationale. This discourse known as the *'Ability and Willingness Paradox in Family Firms'* has opened up an interesting prospect for theory building by offering a theoretical link between family-centric goals such as SEW, collective behaviour of the family firm owners, and firm-centric outcomes such as business performance (Daspit et al., 2021).

Divergent views in the literature highlighted in the previous section triggered the emergence of a new theorem labelled as the 'Ability and Willingness Paradox' (Chrisman et al., 2015; De Massis et al., 2015). Family business scholars agree that as a result of highly concentrated family ownership in the firm and the power to exert control over firm's resource allocation, family business owners typically have high levels of ability to exert control and influence over the strategic and operational decisions of family firms related to strategic decisions such as investing in R&D. However, the proponents of the 'Ability and Willingness Paradox' postulate that family firms have varying levels of willingness to exercise such ability to influence decisions.

The above idea was unravelled through a study on the variation in levels of willingness of family business owners to invest in research and development aimed at driving innovation. The lack of willingness to invest in innovation is driven by socioemotional wealth preservation considerations (Chrisman et al., 2015). The *'Ability and Willingness Paradox'* is an uncomplicated but a powerful theorem that explains the heterogeneity in family firm behaviour by integrating family-centric non-economic parameters along with the willingness perspective next to the ability view into existing discourse in family business research. It must be recognized that some of the earlier studies did allude to this variation in willingness and ability dilemma (e.g. Chrisman & Patel, 2012), however, the idea was given shape and introduced to serious academic discourse by De Massis et al. (2013).

The contribution by De Massis et al. (2013) presents a theoretical framework on how the behaviour of family firm managers and their strategic decisions are influenced by involvement of the family members in key decision-making in such firms. Using the example of policies regarding investing in R&D in family firms, they examine behaviours based on discretion of the family business leaders to act (*Ability*) and their disposition to act (*Willingness*), as the core drivers that create a distinction between family enterprises from non-family ones, and suggest that this variation contributes to heterogeneity among family-owned businesses (Daspit et al., 2021). The word *'paradox'* is used because, while family-firm owners usually have superior ability to execute their goals, yet they often manifest lower levels of desire or willingness to engage in firm performance-centric activities such as investing in diversification, technological innovation, venturing into international markets, and professionalisation of the governance systems. Deciphering this paradox could yield new insights to a better understanding of heterogeneity of family firms and their idiosyncratic behaviours.

In a seminal article on behaviour of family business owners by psychologist Kets de Vries (1993), the author points out that the willingness of the family for continued involvement in the firm and future trans-generational control intentions varies between families based on their circumstances and realities. For example, founders who do not have any children or competent legal heirs may decide to let the business move into the hands of more professional outsiders, and the family gradually starts to resemble a non-family organisation. The firm becomes a source of income for the family and not an arena for translating other social or emotional goals of the family. The above discussion was elaborated on subsequently by other scholars, and especially highlighted in an article by Professor Pramodita Sharma (one of the most prominent family business scholars and the founding editor of the prestigious journal; *Family Business Review*). This *'Ability and Willingness Gap'* was subsequently developed into a theoretical paradigm by De Massis et al. (2014). The argument is pertinent to this study and deserves special attention, as it may be a vital piece of information missing in explaining the heterogeneity among family firms.

The paradox is manifested by family firms in firm-oriented strategic choices such as not wanting to invest in R&D (Chrisman & Patel, 2012) or reluctance to internationalise their firms (Calabro et al., 2013), or tendency to avoid joining cooperatives because they may lose control (Gomez-Mejia et al., 2007) despite having the ability to do so. However, the paradox referred to is complex in nature due to the fact that association between ability and willingness varies in types and levels among different family enterprises. As a result, the outcome of the interaction between ability and willingness varies between firms and is often challenging to predict.

The above paradoxical phenomenon may be attributed to a certain extent to 'ability to control' and 'capacity to control' by family managers, since willingness to manifest controllability may depend on the perceived efficacy of taking such actions. Thus, the tendency among family members involved in the management of the family firm to commit to the firm to further their family-centric goals may be dependent on the level of importance assigned by the family to their socioemotional wealth goals (De Massis et al., 2016). For instance, although control is a major concern for most family business organisations, the balance between concerns for short-term control intentions and long-term control intentions may lead to significantly different propensities to remain actively involved in a firm's strategic and operational decisions (Umans et al., 2019).

Besides the points mentioned above, other factors that are likely to contribute to this ability and willingness gap are personal and circumstantial parameters such as environmental inputs, family conflicts, resource availability, succession and control transfer issues, and possibly many other factors that have not been studied yet, which are drivers of such variations in willingness among family business owner-managers and collective vision of family firm owners that change over time much more so than non-family firms. Chrisman et al. (2014) have pointed out two drivers of the ability and willingness gap '*trans-generational succession intentions*' and '*performance aspirations*'.

4 Family Commitment

In the highly cited study by Anderson and Reeb (2003), the authors determined that among publicly listed companies in the United States, the companies controlled by families on average outperformed the non-family ones. One of the major reasons attributed to this finding is that family business owners have a long-term commitment to the family enterprise, which is often referred to as family commitment. Carlock and Ward (2001), through their seminal piece of work on strategic planning in the family business, elaborately laid out the concept of '*Family Commitment*' in the context of family firms. The process of exploring family commitment requires the family to consider two questions. Firstly, does the family have a collective interest in remaining a family-controlled firm? Secondly, is the controlling family able and willing to accept the responsibilities that go with being the dominant owners of a business organisation? Presence of family commitment requires an affirmative response to both questions, because it entails continuous commitment of resources, effort, and time to the enterprise. The arguments made in the previous section on 'Ability and Willingness Paradox' supports the likelihood that a family may continue to have controlling ownership of the firm, and yet decide not to fully commit to the firm's business goals. Extant literature on family ownership and involvement indicates that absence of active participation in effective governance, leads to a decline in financial performance (Razzak & Jassem, 2019).

Family commitment to the firm is what makes the enterprise a family business. Without a commitment to simultaneously strategize and follow up on the family- and firm-centric goals, there would be no difference between a family firm and a non-family one (Daspit et al., 2021). Without a shared commitment of the family to invest resources, time and effort to the business, subsequent generations of family members may be inclined to selling or liquidating their holdings in the family firm (Umans et al., 2019). Ensuring that family members are dedicated to the family enterprise beyond the founder generation is a daunting task and probably one of the key success factors in keeping the flavour of family-owned business still alive in the organisation. It demands visionary family leadership from the family principles to develop such collaborative vision and pass it on to subsequent generations of family members. However, as the family grows and the family network expands along with marital ties, the cohesion of the family faces challenges, especially when the organisation becomes removed from the founding entrepreneurs.

The example of the Ford family is an excellent anecdote of a strong commitment to the business that bears their family name and how the family managed to perpetuate their vision and values through generations of family firm owners and managers. Henry Ford is known as the founder of the modern mass production automobile industry and the company he founded; the Ford Motor Company that has transformed into a giant transnational company with presence in many regions of the world. Despite the fact that they are among the largest industrial corporation in the world, the Ford family still owns about 40 percent of stock holdings and therefore dominant voting rights, which is enough to ensure their control of one of the largest publicly listed firms (Muller, 2017). William Ford shares the entrepreneurial flare and commitment of his great-grandfather and recognises the unique challenges he is likely to face. He was often seen driving around in newly designed prototypes such as the electric truck, which is expected to be in production soon. When elevated to the position of chairman, he articulated his vision and personal commitment to the family firm by saying, '*I want to serve this company to the best of my ability. The Ford Motor Company is my heritage and has always been a part of my life*' (Muller, 2017).

From the above example, we note that commitment calls for something beyond a mere pledge of loyalty to the enterprise. In fact, it involves a deep and active connection with the firm such that family managers are willing to give a good part of their lives in order to contribute to the firm's well-being. Family commitment is an important variable in comprehending behaviour and organisational relationships. According to Tajpour et al. (2021), commitment to the family firm is based on at least three (3) key factors:

(i) Passionate belief and connection to the goals and visions of the family enterprise.
(ii) A strong desire and willingness to contribute to the family firm.
(iii) Intention for a life-long connection with the organisation.

The above discourse indicates that a crucial element of commitment is behaviour supportive of the organisation's business goals, not mere passing loyalty.

Carlock and Ward (2001) state: '*Family commitment is based on exploring core values, clarifying a family business philosophy and creating a future vision of the family. There are two equally important elements in the commitment decision: maintaining enough ownership to control the firm (ability) and the willingness to participate and accept the responsibilities of active ownership*' *(pg. 55)*. The latter part of the above quote refers to presence of 'willingness' of the family to commit to the organisations' business performance goals, which has been elaborately presented in the preceding section while discussing the discourse on the 'Ability and Willingness Paradox'.

According to Carlock and Ward (2001), family commitment comprises three key elements: (i) the core values the family adheres to with regards to their firm, (ii) the philosophy to be followed in the business, and (iii) the shared future vision of the family. The authors state that these elements are not static, as they are continually influenced by changes within the family and business environment. The family's consensus on these three elements forms the basis for long-term commitment to the family enterprise (Tajpour et al., 2021). The following sub-sections present an overview of the three elements of family commitment mentioned above:

(i) *Family Core Values*:

The family's core values determine shared beliefs about the goals of the family and how they would interact with their business organisation. The family's commitment and vision of itself are determined by what the principles of the family collectively hold as important. The manner in which the family intends to see their employees and customers being treated and how the family principles perceive their responsibilities towards other stakeholders of their enterprise will guide the development of business plans, policies, and family agreements. Therefore, core shared values of the family, especially among the key decision makers are the foundations for developing a commitment to the firm.

(ii) *Philosophy adopted by the Family with regard to the Firm*:

A tacit agreement among family principles on business philosophy to be adopted in governing the firm is closely related to the core values discussed earlier. During family meetings regarding the business, family members often follow a consistent pattern of narratives on issues related to the family's interaction with the firm. Family business philosophy is related to establishing a guiding compass for decision-making such as whether the family considers 'family first' or 'business first' within the organisation.

The business-first approach would obviously prioritize decisions that will be in the best interest of the organisation, which includes firm's customers, employees, and other stakeholders. In such instances, the family is likely to adopt a more professional approach to governance and management in matters such as recruitment, compensation, promotion, supplier selection, and quality control. The expected reasoning would be that principles based on fairness and accountability would be for the long-term sustainability of the firm, where tough decisions taken may affect short-term interests of the family. The family members are collectively willing to abide by these principles and show tolerance even if they lead to perceptions of unfairness.

On the other hand, the family-first approach is based on the premise that the family's priorities such as happiness, harmony, and economic well-being should dominate all other considerations. This would mean that business decisions consistently favour family-centric priorities, even if there is a trade-off with the firm's financial interests. The outcome of such philosophy is that despite contributions to the business and individual performance, all family members will be provided more or less similar benefits. Such family firms will allow almost every interested family member to be employed by the organisation and be given priority over non-family employees. Practically it would be rare to see any family member terminated or removed from management no matter how they behave. Such family firm owners believe that their family-first philosophy is important, even if they have negative long-term implications for the firm. The source of this philosophy is that the enterprise cannot stay healthy, unless the family members are content and are united in supporting the current family managers in leadership of the firm.

The research framework in this study aims to shed light on the apparent conflict between the two, and attempts to pave the path for family firm decision makers to balance between the 'business first' and the 'family first' camps. The idea holds that any decision must provide for both the well-being of the family and the health of the business. Only under such conditions can a company thrive and stay in the family well into the future. Only an appropriate balance between the two will win the commitment of the family and support for the business. Family members who hold this view believe that abusing the needs of either family or business will damage the future. Therefore, family enterprises require an approach that implies a long-term commitment to the future of the business and family goals, requiring the family principles to search for creative compromises between the two interests.

(iii) *Shared Future Vision*:

A shared future vision among family firm owners is an important factor because it brings focus of the family decision makers to future goals rather than on current challenges. '*For family firms, the shared future vision of the family and business is a linkage between the systems, which expresses their mutual interdependence and the power of their combined efforts*' (Carlock & Ward, 2001: pg. 55).

The family's shared future vision serves multiple functions such as providing new information about future directions, inducing motivation and optimism, giving impetus to the strategic planning process, providing guidelines for policy decisions, and leading to a broad consensus among family principles on the shared future vision (Chrisman et al., 2015). As a result, the business plans drawn up by family managers reflect these broad expectations of the family's ensuring long-term support. When the family network grows larger and the number of family members in ownership and/or management functions increases, it then becomes imperative to organise formal strategic planning and policy meetings among family members and top management teams to forge and maintain a mutually supported future vision.

Commitment to the family organisation in the form of family control facilitates stewardship behaviour. This stewardship behaviour of family-managers results from a sense of psychological ownership, resulting in deep commitment to the mission and vision of the firm, which creates a frame of mind that the success of the family enterprise must be achieved even at the cost of personal sacrifices. Consequence of such deep emotional ties to the firm may lead to alignment of the family goals with the goals of the business enterprise (Tajpour et al., 2021).

5 The Sultanate of Oman

The Sultanate of Oman is the third largest country in the Arabian Peninsula with a land area of about 212,460 square kilometres. It shares land borders with the Kingdom of Saudi Arabia, Yemen, and the United Arab Emirates (UAE), and the remaining border is coastline with the Indian Ocean, the Gulf of Oman, and the Arabian Gulf. Oman is one of the members of the GCC (Gulf Cooperation Council) (Islam, 2020).

The six (6) member GCC countries share a common language and religion; Arabic and Islam, respectively. However, in terms of history, Oman is among the oldest civilisations, especially in the Dhofar region of the country is home to many ancient civilisations. Strategically, Oman is situated in one of the most crucial trade routes in the world, the Hormuz Strait, which is the essential lifeline to the world's crude oil supply. Topologically, Oman is different from other GCC countries, as it has monsoon-type weather in its' south, and a vast array of mountain ranges that rise to nearly 3000 metres. Culturally, it has a rich mix that resulted from its' heritage derived from its' multiple tribal values, and its' Arab, Zanzibari, and Balochi cultures. In terms of religious practices, the Omanis strongly value their Islamic culture, but are extremely tolerant to others (Kothaneth, 2019).

Oman as a nation is considered among the oldest of the civilisations in the Arab world. Evidence unearthed by western archaeologists indicates that the ancient city of Al Wattih, which was in Oman, dates to over 10,000 years. Historians note that pre-Islamic Oman was dominated by Babylonians, Assyrians, and the Persian Empire, because of its' strategic location on the Indian Ocean. The advent of the Islamic era started during the period of the Holy Prophet Muhammad (May Allah's Peace and Blessings be Upon him) in the early seventh century AD In fact, a letter from the Prophet Muhammad is exhibited in the National Museum in Oman, which invites the Omani people to Islam and mentions a prayer *'Allah's mercy be on the people of Al Ghubaira (Oman), they believed in me although they have not seen me'* (Kothaneth, 2019).

Subsequently, Oman has been ruled by various dynasties, imamates (rule of imams or khalifahs through oath of allegiance), and foreign powers including the Persians, the Portuguese, and the British. The longest-serving dynasty was the Nathania dynasty that ruled till 1470. By the eighteenth century, the empire stretched until the East African Coast of Zanzibar. The Al-Said dynasty has been ruling Oman from 1744 to present. After 1970, when Sultan Qaboos bin Said took over the reins of the country, a new era of development and modernisation had taken root in the Sultanate of Oman (Landen, 2015; Risso, 2016).

Oman has been fortunate with the discovery of large deposits of oil and gas, making it a member of a small league of wealthy nations known as the GCC. Compared to the other five GCC member nations both Oman and Bahrain's annual revenues from oil and gas are considerably lower. Furthermore, the ratio of Omani citizens to foreign workers is much higher than its' neighbours. For instance, in Qatar and UAE, the composition of local citizens to foreigners is considerably low, while in Oman majority of population are Omani citizens. This may be considered a boon for Oman both in terms of having a sustainable demographic mix, as well as from point of view of national security (Mahi & Thani, 2019).

6 Business Ecosystem

The Late Sultan Qaboos ruled for five decades, and he was revered by his people as well as by foreigners residing in Oman. He was a highly educated and enlightened man, whose priority was the prosperity and safety of his people. The discovery of fossil fuel and windfall profits from the sale of hydrocarbons enabled the country to transform itself from the past into a modern nation that is also deeply rooted in its' traditions (Mahi & Thani, 2019). However, over the last decade, the Late Sultan Qaboos knew that he had to induce a second economic revolution to enable his nation into an economically diversified and highly capable diaspora to meet the challenges of the future. With these goals in mind, Oman declared the Oman Vision 2040, where entrepreneurship development was a vital component. Within the framework of the Oman Vision 2040, is the underlying theme of Omanisation. The Omanisation program not only aims at replacing foreign workers with Omani citizens but also emphasizes growth in business ownership among under-represented parts of society such as women. For driving the entrepreneurship development agenda, the government has created a body known as Tanfeedh. The new economic mission under the Oman Vision 2040 is being fully implemented under the able leadership of the present sultan, His Majesty Haitham bin Tariq (Al Sinani et al., 2021).

Under the ninth five-year plan for National Program for Enhancing Economic Diversification (Tanfeedh), the development of an entrepreneurial ecosystem has been given high priority. The Omani government has considered enhancing the role of the private sector as an engine of GDP growth. In this situation, the focus of the government has shifted towards SMEs (small and medium enterprises), which involves strategic plans along with numerous project initiatives. The programmes were developed after examining the best practices of industrialised nations with more or less similar demography, which have successfully diversified their economies through entrepreneurship and SME development. Such ecosystems capture different factors of entrepreneurship development at both macroeconomic and microeconomic levels. Key individuals who are tasked with executing Tanfeedh are working to update the entrepreneurial ecosystems in Oman to achieve the goal of economic diversity (Sanyal & Hisam, 2018).

7 Family Businesses

Oman is a collectivist society where close family bonds go hand in hand with its' indigenous culture. As a result, the social fabric of Oman makes it a fertile ground for development of family-owned businesses. Surprisingly very few empirically sound published materials are presently available on the prevailing situation with family firms in Oman (Gupta, 2021). Majority of the academic research publications in the context of family businesses in Oman are not very recent and are based on certain rural and coastal parts of the country. For instance, Belwal et al. (2014) conducted a study on the Al-Dhahirah region, while Al-Sadi et al. (2011) looked at the Al-Batinah region, Chaudhry et al. (2018) conducted a study on the Sharqiyah region, and Sanyal (2014) conducted their study on the coastal region of Dhofar, which is also the southernmost province of the country bordering Yemen.

Among the few studies covering the capital city of Muscat is by McElwee and Al-Riyami (2003), which was published nearly 19 years ago. Hence, there appears to be a dearth of sufficient peer-reviewed recent publications on the overall situation with family firms in Oman. One of the reasons that may be attributed to a lack of sufficient recent academic studies on family firms in Oman is that the policymakers and academics in the country have been emphasising development of SMEs and entrepreneurship as a part of the Oman Vision 2040, and not exclusively focusing on family businesses (Gupta, 2021). This tendency is probably because there is an assumption that SMEs automatically mean family-owned businesses. The reality is that family firms derive their distinctive nature from the fact that the goals of the family and the business are both important to the owners. Hence, SMEs may include family firms, but it does not automatically mean that all SMEs have the flavour of a family-owned business.

Despite the paucity of academic literature in the context of family businesses in Oman, some useful information is available from reports published by reputed international consulting firms such as McKinsey & Company, KPMG, and PricewaterhouseCoopers (KPMG, 2015; McKinsey & Company, 2019; PwC Report, 2021). The PwC report indicates that approximately 93% of the businesses in Oman, whether large or small are controlled by a single family or a coalition of families. These firms may be categorised into large, medium, small, and micro-enterprises. The following subsections provide further details on the categories.

7.1 Large Family Firms in Oman

Based on a list published by the Forbes magazine on the Top 100 Family Businesses in the Middle East, five (5) of them are Omani large family-owned companies that feature on this list. These companies are listed in ascending order from the largest in terms of annual turnover: (i) Suhail Bahwan Group (SBG), (ii) Zubair Corporation, (iii) Saud Bahwan Group, (iv) WJ Towell & Company, and the (v) Mohsin Haider Darwish Group (Forbes, 2021 May).

The Suhail Bahwan Group is the largest of all family-owned businesses in Oman. Suhail Bahwan and his brother Saud Bahwan founded it in 1965. The brothers were small traders in the Muttrah Souq, which is the oldest marketplace in Muscat. The group now controls 30 companies with over 7000 employees. The company represents some of the iconic global brands such as Toshiba, Mitsubishi, and Epson. Furthermore, the group is involved in fertilisers and chemicals, and owns a large stake in the National Bank of Oman. The estimated value of the company is around USD $ 2.3 Billion (Forbes, 2021).

The Zubair Corporation is the second largest family firm in Oman. Mohammad Al Zubair founded the organisation in 1976. The group has multiple divisions ranging from energy, automobiles, financial services, logistics, hospitality, manufacturing, and real estate. The automotive division represents brands such as Chrysler, Dodge, and Jeep in Oman. The family also owns controlling shares of Ominvest, which is the largest private investment company in the country. Furthermore, the company is currently involved in the development of one of the largest real estate projects in the country. Forbes estimates the value of the company at USD $ 1.9 Billion (Forbes, 2021).

The Saud Bahwan Group was formed after Mohammad Saud Bahwan split from his brother Suhail Bahwan in 2002. The company employs over 10,000 people and represents some major global brands such as Toyota and Komatsu in Oman. Besides automobiles, the company is involved in real estate, construction, and tourism. The value of the company has been estimated to be around USD $ 1.77 Billion (Forbes, 2021).

Mohsin Haider Darwish is the fourth largest family-owned business in Oman. The Late Mohsin Haider Darwish founded it in 1987. Presently the daughters of the late founder, Areej Mohsin Darwish and Lujiana Mohsin Darwish, manage the group. The company represents brands such as Huawei, Honeywell, Nokia, Jaguar, Volvo, and McLaren in Oman. Furthermore, the group is involved in electronics, engineering, construction, and building materials. The value of the company is estimated to be around USD $ 1.2 Billion (Forbes, 2021).

The fifth largest family firm in Oman by company size is the WJ Towell and Company. This company was originally founded in 1866 during the British occupation of this part of the world. However, Late Mohammed Fadhil purchased the company in 1914. It is now a wholly owned Omani company. The group has multiple business divisions that represent multinational brands in Oman such as Unilever, Nestle among others. The group also has operations in many countries within the Middle East and outside including Africa and India. The estimated value of the company is around USD $ 980 Million (Forbes, 2021).

Besides the above large Omani family business groups, there are several other family-owned Omani companies that may be classified in the range of medium to large-sized organisations. However, most of the large commercial organisations in Oman are either owned by the government or are publicly listed companies and many of them are owned by non-Omani entities from UAE, Kuwait, Qatar, and Saudi Arabia (Al-Maskari et al., 2019).

7.2 Micro, Small, and Medium-Sized Family Firms in Oman

The definition of micro, small, and medium enterprises in Oman has been delineated by the Public Authority of SME Development (PASMED), which is a body under the Ministry of Commerce. Table 1 displays the classification of organisations in Oman based on number of employees and annual turnover.

Although there appears to be no additional data on any of the government websites or official reports published by PASMED or any other ministry on how many of these organisations are family-owned businesses, two studies published by consulting firms KPMG in 2015 and then by PwC in 2021 indicate that based on random sampling, about 93% of such micro- and SMEs in Oman are created by families and are operated by either a single family or a coalition of families (KPMG, 2015; PwC, 2021). Considering that the above information is a fairly accurate depiction on the position of family firms within the domain of micro and SMEs in the Sultanate of Oman, it appears that overwhelming majority of these businesses are family owned. However, PASMED or any official government body does not seem to make any distinction between such enterprises and family firms.

Despite the paucity of information through peer-reviewed literature, there are numerous case studies developed by graduate students on Omani family-owned businesses in the library archives of major public universities and colleges in Oman. Many of these case studies traditional medium-sized family firms are well-known local brands such as Hilia, Amouage Perfumery, and Al Hosni Sweets

Table 1 Classification of enterprises in Oman based on firm size

No.	Size	Number of employees	Annual turnover (Omani Riyals)
1	Micro	1–4	<25,000
2	Small	5–9	25,000 to <250,000
3	Medium	10–99	250,000 to <1,500,000

Source: Website of Ministry of Commerce

Family Business in Oman

Exhibit 1 Founder of Hilia Nasser bin Saif Al Tiwani and Sons with the Silver Khanjars *Source: Photograph provided by the Family*

(Al-Lawati et al., 2021). Many of these businesses are now into their third generation of successors.

For instance, Hilia is one of the most recognised local brands in Oman. The company makes *khanjars* (daggers), which are part of the Omani traditional attire for men (Fig. 1). The silver daggers of this company are in high demand and are handcrafted. The business was started by Mr. Nasser bin Saif Al-Tiwani in 1980, and now involves all the sons of the founder. The 'khanjars'[1] are highly prized and are ordered by the royalty in Oman, and other countries in the Middle East. The company has sales showrooms in Saudi Arabia, Qatar, and UAE. The family takes a lot of pride in the production process of each khanjar (Chaudhry et al., 2018). Exhibit 1 shows two generations of the family firm leaders.

Another interesting story is the case of Amouage Perfumery. This Omani company was set up in 1983 to develop a local company that caters to the perfume loving people of Oman. The company developed unique packaging for perfumes that had fragrances that go with the preferences of the Arabs in the GCC region. The product development and quality control of this company were remarkable, and their

---

[1] Khajnars are traditional knifes in Oman used during various ceremonies.

Exhibit 2 Amouage, the retail outlet at the City Centre of Muscat, Seeb. *Source: Mohammad Rezaur Razzak*

packaging is innovative and unique. For instance, drawing from Chinese cinema and Shanghai Deco, Amouage designed bottles for one of its' popular fragrances with a deep red coating with 24-carat gold caps. The products sold by this company are often more expensive than many of the top international perfume brands and are displayed in their exclusive showrooms in such manner (Exhibit 2). This product differentiation strategy has worked well for the company, and the company's brand is highly regarded by Omanis and foreigners, thus generating substantial operating profits for the company (Exhibit 4). The outstanding product design drew attention from top business magazines such as Forbes that published an article on the company in 2015 (Wu, 2014).

Another family-owned SME is Al Hosni Omani Sweets. It was founded in the 1950s by Ali bin Suleiman Al Hosni who started his business in Zanzibar. The region of Zanzibar, which is now part of Tanzania in East Africa, was previously a colony of the Sultanate of Oman. The family business in Zanzibar was named *Halwa Home* and was quite a popular brand that made exotic sweets that were liked by Arabs of Omani origin living in Zanzibar. In the 1970s when Sultan Qaboos ascended to the throne, he encouraged Omani businesspeople in Zanzibar to move back to Oman to develop the country. At that time, the children of the founder decided to move their flourishing business to Muscat. The company was re-branded as Al Hosni Omani Sweets that has become one of the most popular brands in Oman with retail outlets all over the country (Al-Lawati et al., 2021). The secret recipe for preparing the various popular brands of halwa is closely guarded by the family and is

Exhibit 3 Keeping the recipe within the Family at Al Hosni. *Source: Mohammad Rezaur Razzak*

passed on from one generation to another (Exhibit 3). The products of this company are ordered in large quantities during festivals and ceremonies such as weddings. The company is now run by the grandson of the founder, Murshid Al Hosni, who pioneered the expansion of the business to neighbouring countries such as UAE and Qatar (Samara, 2021).

7.3 Influence of Omani Culture on Family Business

Indigenous culture has idiosyncratic influence on the focus and behaviour of a family of family-firm owners (Al-Maskari et al., 2019). In the case of Oman, the behaviour of family businesses standout in two areas: *practice of primogeniture* and *empathy towards non-family employees* (Chaudhury & Sultan, 2017).

7.3.1 Succession Right of the First Born

The Italian family business scholar, Andrea Calabro and colleagues conducted an interesting study on the practice of *primogeniture* in the context of family firm succession and subsequent performance of such firms over time in the region of

Sardinia in the Southern part of Italy (Calabro et al., 2018). Primogeniture is the practice among many cultures about '*the right of the first born to be the successor*'. The findings revealed by the above study indicate that most family firms that are led by the eldest child from the founders, tend to show a significant decline in performance compared to their predecessors. Calabro and colleagues also discovered that it is usually the third child that performs the best as the next family-firm leader. The practice of primogeniture is also quite relevant to the Omani society also. In fact, the matter is taken a step further by many Omani family firms by assuming that the right to succession belongs to the first-born *male* child. Being a paternalistic culture, men are automatically expected to carry the mantle from their predecessors. As a result over decades women had played a lesser role in running family businesses in Oman, although over the last few years many Omani women are seen in top management of large family businesses. In terms of how this practice in Oman aligns with the findings of Calabro et al. (2018) with regards to firm performance, maybe an interesting research opportunity for future.

7.3.2 Empathy as a Resource of Organisational Resilience

A unique cultural aspect of family firms in Oman is related to the benevolent nature of the Omani people. Outsiders who have interacted with the people in Oman find them to be generally gentle and empathetic. This nature of Omanis seems to also be reflected in the realm of family-owned businesses when it comes to treatment of non-family employees, especially those who are migrant workers. There are sufficient anecdotal evidence to support the notion that family business owners in Oman run their businesses with a mix of goal for business performance along with caring for employees (McKinsey & Company, 2019).

The preceding phenomenon was manifested in the case of many organisations at the height of the COVID-19 pandemic from 2020 to 2021. For instance, the Moon Group is a medium-sized Omani company with three companies that operate in travel and tourism, maintenance services of buildings and infrastructure, and courier services. From March 2020 onwards when the Omani authorities to control the spread of infections imposed severe social distancing measures, most of the group's revenues were at a standstill. Particularly, both the travel and the tourism along with building maintenance services were practically on hold. The only company that was generating income was the courier service because of their connection with e-commerce companies. At that time, the owner Mr. Khalfan Al-Aufi, had the option of terminating all redundant non-family employees or keeping them on the payroll for an indefinite period, as the end of the pandemic was not visible in the horizon at that time. After lengthy deliberations with other family members involved with the business, the owners decided to approach their employees to take a moratorium on their monthly salaries till things return to normalcy or the company finds a way out. During this time, the company would provide accommodation and food to all employees, and put their salary payments as accounts payable till they had sufficient liquidity to start paying of overdue salaries in the future. Almost all employees were relieved and agreed to support the company's proposal. Such examples are rare in the case of non-family firms, and also outside such cultures where protection of people's livelihoods is considered sacred (Khan et al., 2020).

Another remarkable example of how family businesses in Oman demonstrate caring for others beyond normal economic logic is the example of Al Hosni Omani Sweets, which was started by Ali bin Al Hosni in the 1950s. Now the business is in the hands of the third-generation family successors. During the pandemic, most retail outlets were shut down and the business with multiple stores around the country and in other GCC countries took a hit. Despite the tremendous pressure on the company's liquidity position, the owners decided to retain their employees by offering them to remain employed with a 50% pay cut till return to normalcy. Some of the employees have been connected with the business for at least two generations, as a result the owners felt reluctant in terminating employees at that time. Such amazing acts of generosity appear to defy economic logic, yet they go hand in hand with the nature of the Omani people and their cultural heritage (Gupta, 2021).

8 Concluding Remarks

It goes without saying that family businesses are one of the prime movers of the national economy in Oman. With the new vision of the rulers in the Sultanate of Oman to diversify the economy from primary reliance on revenues from oil and gas exports to an economy that is driven by growth of private enterprise through entrepreneurship, the emphasis on the role of family businesses needs to be taken into consideration. At present, the focus of the authorities who are entrusted with managing the changes in the economy are on the development of small and medium enterprises (SMEs) through multiple programs and projects. For instance, high priority has been attached to entrepreneurial education in tertiary-level education. The aim is to encourage students to create their own jobs rather than seek employment. Another noteworthy initiative is to drive innovation among public and private sector organisations. Other programmes are aimed at technical education for skill development, business incubation through start-up hubs, facilities for providing entrepreneurship training to women and to rural communities etc.

The initiatives mentioned in the preceding paragraph are all expected to contribute to the development of private sector-driven business development and growth. However, what appears to be missing is any specially dedicated programme that places emphasis on family-owned businesses. The discourses presented in the earlier sections on socioemotional wealth, ability and willingness paradox, and family commitment demonstrate that looking at family firms with a completely different lens is imperative. Organisations that are family controlled will prioritise socioemotional wealth and thus demonstrate idiosyncratic behaviour that is related to the tendency of family-firm owners to give preference to their non-economic family-centred goals. Furthermore, family firms have the ability to make long-term commitments to the sustainability of the enterprise that may be a source of their competitiveness and survival capital. Therefore, for policymakers and regulatory authorities entrusted with driving development and growth of entrepreneurial ventures in Oman, it is important to take into cognizance the essential features that drive intentions, goals, and behaviour of family businesses. Without the above realisation, programmes and initiatives aimed at driving development and sustainability of private business enterprises may be misdirected and ineffective.

In addition to the above, the cultural factors that drive the behaviour of Omani family firms are also to be taken into consideration. For instance, the practice of preferring the first-born male child as the successor to the leadership of the business without considering the most qualified and capable individual is a matter that needs to be looked at. Although such practices are embedded in the customs and norms of the society, however, through proper communication and education of new generation of family business managers, eventually with time more objective analysis of an appropriate selection of suitable successors may be possible. On the other hand, positive behaviours of Omani family business owners that emanate from their culture such as empathy towards non-family employees may be encouraged. Such benevolent actions of family firms towards people who work for them may appear to be economically irrational in the short term, yet they can become a source of organisational resilience that is created through employee loyalty and performance.

This chapter starts with a general discussion on the core elements that distinguish family-owned businesses from those that do not fall into the category of a family business. The areas identified from the academic literature are based on priority attached to socioemotional wealth, the ability and willingness paradox, and family commitment as a source of competitive advantage and organisational resilience. Thereafter, some general overviews about Oman, its history and the prevailing business ecosystem are presented. The following section delves into some factors that standout among Omani family firms as a result of the cultural context in the country. The first of these factors is about selecting the first-born male child as the likely successor to the incumbent leaders in the family business. The other factor is a general manifestation of caring and empathy towards all employees whether they are family- or non-family employees. It is anticipated that the aforesaid discussions will present a unique view about family businesses in Oman.

References

Al Sinani, A. Z. M., Ayyapan, P., & Magd, H. (2021). Corporate governance best practices aligned with Oman Vision 2040–way forward. *Global Business and Management Research, 13*(3), 57–69.

Al-Lawati, E. H., Kohar, U. H. A., & Bin Suleiman, E. S. (2021). Entrepreneurship studies in the Sultanate of Oman: A scoping review of 20 years publications. *Applied Economics, 30*(1), 238–252.

Al-Maskari, A., Al-Maskari, M., Alqanoobi, M., & Kunjumuhammed, S. (2019). Internal and external obstacles facing medium and large enterprises in Rusayl Industrial Estates in the Sultanate of Oman. *Journal of Global Entrepreneurship Research, 9*(1), 1–20.

Al-Sadi, R., Belwal, R., & Al-Badi, R. (2011). Woman entrepreneurship in the Al-Batinah region of Oman: An identification of the barriers. *Journal of International Women's Studies, 12*(3), 58–75.

Anderson, R., & Reeb, D. (2003). Founding-family ownership and firm performance: Evidence from the S&P 500. *Journal of Finance, 58*(3), 1301–1327.

Belwal, S., Belwal, R., & Al Saidi, F. (2014). Characteristics, motivations and challenges of women entrepreneurs in Oman's Al-Dhahira region. *Journal of Middle East Women's Studies, 10*(2), 135–151.

Berrone, P., Cruz, C., & Gomez-Mejia, L. R. (2012). Socioemotional wealth in family firms theoretical dimensions, assessment approaches, and agenda for future research. *Family Business Review, 25*(3), 258–279.

Bringham, K., & Payne, G. T. (2019). Socioemotional wealth (SEW): Questions on construct validity. *Family Business Review, 32*(4), 326–329.

Calabro, A., Minichilli, A., Amore, M. D., & Brogi, M. (2018). The courage to choose! Primogeniture and leadership succession in family firms. *Strategic Management Journal, 39*(7), 2014–2035.

Calabro, A., Torchia, M., Pukall, T., & Mussolino, D. (2013). The influence of ownership structure and board strategic involvement on international sales: The moderating effect of family involvement. *International Business Review, 22*(3), 509–523.

Carlock, R. S., & Ward, J. L. (2001). *Strategic planning for the family business: Parallel planning to unify the family and business*. Houndsmill.

Chaudhry, I. S., Al Harthy, S., Al Shibli, S., Sultan, N., & Maurice, J. G. (2018). Family-based enterprises in North-Sharqiyah region of Oman: Opportunities and challenges. *Middle East Journal of Management, 10*(1), 332–348.

Chaudhury, I. S., & Sultan, N. (2017). Family-based enterprises in North-Sharqiyah region of Oman: Opportunities and challenges. *Middle East Journal of Management, 4*(3), 246–260.

Chrisman, J. J., & Patel, P. C. (2012). Variations in R&D investments of family and non- family firms: Behavioral agency and myopic loss aversion perspectives. *Academy of Management Journal, 55*(4), 976–997.

Chrisman, J. J., & Holt, D. T. (2016). Beyond socioemotional wealth: Taking another step toward a theory of the family firm. *Management Research: Journal of the Iberoamerican Academy of Management, 14*(3), 279–287.

Chrisman, J. J., Memilli, E., & Misra, K. (2014). Nonfamily managers, family firms, and the winner's curse: The influence of noneconomic goals and bounded rationality. *Entrepreneurship Theory & Practice, 38*(5), 120–141.

Chrisman, J. J., Chua, J. H., De Massis, A., Frattini, F., & Wright, M. (2015). The ability and willingness paradox in family firm innovation. *Journal of Product Innovation Management, 32*(3), 310–318.

Daspit, J. J., Chrisman, J. J., Ashton, T., & Evangelopoulos, N. (2021). Family firm heterogeneity: A definition, common themes, scholarly Progress, and directions forward. *Family Business Review, 34*(3), 296–322.

De Massis, A., Di Minin, A., & Frattini, F. (2015). Family-driven innovation: Resolving the paradox in family firms. *California Management Review, 58*(1), 5–19.

De Massis, A., Kotlar, J., Campopiano, G., & Cassia, L. (2013). Dispersion of family ownership and the performance of small-to-medium size private family firms. *Journal of Business Strategy, 4*(3), 166–175.

De Massis, A., Kotlar, J., Chua, J. H., & Chrisman, J. J. (2014). Ability and willingness as sufficiency conditions for family-oriented particularistic behavior: Implications for theory and empirical studies. *Journal of Small Business Management, 52*(2), 344–364.

De Massis, A., Frattini, F., Kotlar, J., Pettruzelli, A. M., & Wright, M. (2016). Innovation through tradition: Lessons from innovative family businesses and directions for future research. *Academy of Management, 30*(1), 105–127.

De Massis, A., Frattini, F., Majocchi, A., & Piscitello, L. (2018). Family firms in the global economy: Toward a deeper understanding of internationalization determinants, processes, and outcomes. *Global Strategy Journal, 8*(1), 3–21.

Ernst, R. A., Gerken, M., Hack, A., & Hulsbeck, M. (2022). Family firms as agents of sustainable development: A normative perspective. *Technological Forecasting and Social Change*, 174 (ahead-of-print).

Forbes. (2021, May). Top 100 Arab Family Businesses in the Middle East. *Forbes online*. Available at: https://www.forbesmiddleeast.com/lists/top-100-arab-family-businesses-in-the-middle-east-2021/

Gerken, M., Hulsbeck, M., Ostermann, T., & Hack, A. (2022). Validating the FIBER scale to measure family firm heterogeneity–a replication study with extensions. *Journal of Family Business Strategy*. (ahead-of-print).

Ghouse, S. M., McElwee, G., & Durrah, O. (2019). Entrepreneurial success of cottage-based women entrepeneurs in Oman. *International Journal of Entrepreneurial Behavior Research, 25*(3), 480–498.

Gomez-Mejia, L. R., Haynes, K. T., Nunez-Nickel, M., Jacobson, K. J. L., & Moyano-Fuentes, J. (2007). Socioemotional wealth and business risks in family-controlled firms: Evidence from Spanish olive oil Mills. *Administrative Science Quarterly, 52*(1), 106–137.

Gomez-Mejia, L. R., & Herreo, I. (2022). Back to square one: The measurement of socioemotional wealth (SEW). *Journal of Family Business Strategy*. (ahead-of-print).

Gupta, S. L. (2021). Perceived motivators and barriers for entrepreneurship: An empirical study of SMEs in Oman. *The Journal of Asian Finance, Economics and Business., 8*(5), 863–872.

Hauck, J., Suess-Reyesm, J., Beck, S., Prügl, R., & Hermann, F. (2016). Measuring socioemotional wealth in family-owned and -managed firms: A validation and short form of the FIBER scale. *Journal of Family Business Strategy, 7*(3), 133–148.

Islam, M. M. (2020). Demographic transition in Sultanate of Oman: Emerging demographic dividend and challenges. *Middle East Fertility Society Journal, 25*(7), 218–239.

Kets de Vries, M. F. R. (1993). The dynamics of family controlled firms: The good and the bad news. *Organizational Dynamics, 21*(3), 59–71.

Khan, G. M., Razzak, M. R., & Al-Aufi, S. K. (2020, November). *Case study presented at international conference "family business in the Arab world"*. American University at Sharjah.

Kothaneth, L. (2019, May). *Islam in Oman: A Precious letter that is pride of nation*. Oman Observer. Retrieved from: https://www.omanobserver.om/article/32249/Features/islam-in-oman-a-precious-letter-that-is-pride-of-the-nation

KPMG (2015). *Family Business in Oman*. KPMG Online Report. Available at: https://home.kpmg/om/en/home/insights/2012/04/family-business-articles.html

Laffranchini, G., Hadjimarcou, J. S., & Kim, S. H. (2018). The impact of socioemotional wealth on decline-stemming strategies of family firms. *Entrepreneurship Theory and Practice, 100*(6), 1–26.

Landen, R.G. (2015). *Oman Since 1856*. Volume 2286 in the series Princeton Legacy Library.

Mahi, S. R., & Thani, J. K. N. A. (2019). The strategies used by SMEs to survuve during economic crisis in the Sultanate of Oman. *Journal of Student Research, 4*, 131–142.

McElwee, G., & Al-Riyami, R. (2003). Women entrepreneurs in Oman: Some barriers to success. *Career Development International, 8*(7), 339–346.

McKinsey & Company. (2019). *Family Business Practice*. McKinsey Report on Family Business in the Middle East. Available at: https://www.mckinsey.com/middle-east/our-work/family-business-practice

Muller, J. (2017, May). In sweeping leadership change, Ford Replaces CEO Mark Fields With James Hackett. *Forbes online*. Available at: https://www.forbes.com/sites/joannmuller/2017/05/22/in-sweeping-leadership-change-ford-replaces-ceo-mark-fields-with-james-hackett/?sh=4c3cfd784784

Prugl, R. (2018). Capturing the heterogeneity of family firms: Reviewing scales to directly measure socioemotional wealth. In E. Memili & C. Dibrell (Eds.), *The Palgrave handbook of heterogeneity among family firms* (pp. 457–480). Palgrave.

PwC Report. (2021). *Diversifying, investing and digitising: Middle East Family Business Survey 2021*. Pricewaterhouse Coopers online report, Available at: https://www.pwc.com/m1/en/publications/middle-east-family-business-survey.html

Razzak, M. R., & Jassem, S. (2019). Socioemotional wealth and performance in private family firms: The mediation effect of family commitment. *Journal of Family Business Management, 9*(4), 468–496.

Risso, P. (2016). *Oman and Muscat*. Routledge.

Samara, G. (2021). Family businesses in the Arab middle east: What do we know and where should we go? *Journal of Family Business Strategy, 12*(1), 100–119.

Sanyal, S. (2014). *Challenges facing entrepreneurs in developing countries: A study of Dhofar region of Sultanate of Oman*. Paper presented in 2nd International Conference on Emerging Trends in Scientific Research.

Sanyal, S., & Hisam, M. W. (2018). The role of business incubators in creating an entrepreneurial ecosystem: A study of the Sultanate of Oman. *Indian Journal of Commerce and Management Studies, 9*(3), 52–67.

Swab, R. G., Sherlock, C., Markin, E., & Dibrell, C. (2020). "SEW" what do we know and where do we go? A review of socioemotional wealth and a way forward. *Family Business Review, 33*(4), 424–445.

Tabor, W., Chrisman, J. J., Madison, K., & Vardaman, J. M. (2017). Nonfamily members in family firms: A review and future agenda. *Family Business Review, 31*(1), 54–79.

Tajpour, M., Salamzadeh, A., Salamzadeh, Y., & Braga, V. (2021). Investigating social capital, trust and commitment in family business: Case of media firms. *Journal of Family Business Management*, ahead-of-print.

Umans, I., Lybaert, N., Steijvers, T., & Voordeckers, W. (2019). The influence of transgenerational succession intentions on the succession planning process: The moderating role of high-quality relationships. *Journal of Family Business Strategy, 12*(2), 35–51.

Wu, S.Y. (2014). Amouage journey: Fall Fragrances for people who love a good scent story. *Forbes online*. Available at: https://www.forbes.com/sites/sarahwu/2014/08/27/amouage-journey-fall-fragrances-for-people-who-love-a-good-scent-story/?sh=31ee9a7e72b6

Mohammad Rezaur Razzak is an Assistant Professor of Strategic Management, Entrepreneurship, and Family Business at the College of Economics & Political Science (EQUIS accredited), at Sultan Qaboos University in Oman. He obtained his bachelor's degree in mechanical engineering from the University of Texas at Austin followed by MBA from Southern Methodist University. He completed his PhD with distinction from the University of Malaya specializing in strategy and family business. Dr. Razzak has over 35 years of experience that includes industrial and corporate positions followed by a full time engagement in academia. At present his research interests are in the areas of family business, digital entrepreneurship, emerging business models in the Industry 4.0 era, and sustainable manufacturing and supply chain practices through digitalization.

Ramo Palalić is an Assistant Professor at the Management Department, College of Economics and Political Science (EQUIS accredited), Sultan Qaboos University (SQU), Oman. His research is in the area of entrepreneurship, leadership, and management. Dr. Palalić has authored and co-authored many articles in globally recognised journals like *Management Decision, International Journal of Entrepreneurial Behavior & Research, International Entrepreneurship and Management Journal*, and alike. Additionally, he has co-authored/co-edited several books and many book chapters in the field of business and entrepreneurship published with internationally prominent publishers (Springer, Routledge, World Scientific). Moreover, Dr. Palalić is serving as the EiC/Associate editors/editor board member in several well-established international journals. Apart from his research, he was involved in business projects in the areas of entrepreneurial leadership and marketing management, in private and public organisations.

Said Al-Riyami is an Assistant Professor and the Head of the Department of Management at the College of Economics & Political Science (EQUIS accredited), at Sultan Qaboos University, Oman. Before joining academia, he worked in different public institutions. Dr. Said obtained his PhD and MBA from the University of Texas at El Paso, USA. He has published a number of articles in Web of Science and Scopus Indexed journals. His main research interests include organisational leadership, job embeddedness, organisational behaviour, and proactivity.

Family Business in Saudi Arabia

Wassim J. Aloulou and Riyadh Alshaeel

Abstract This chapter aims to provide an understanding of the dynamics of family business phenomenon in Saudi Arabia. In its *introduction*, the chapter starts by providing a general information about the main characteristics of the country and its performance in terms of development, growth, and value. In its *first part*, the chapter presents an overview of the business and entrepreneurial ecosystem of family businesses in Saudi Arabia. In the *second part*, the chapter deepens the view of the family business phenomenon in Saudi Arabia, its importance, and key success factors in the GCC region. In its *third part*, the chapter opens new perspectives of the phenomenon by renewing it through fostering entrepreneurship outside the family business and empowering the role of women as leaders in Saudi family business. *In the end*, the chapter gives certain concluding remarks about how to sustain the family business phenomenon from one generation to another in the country and how to pursue its contribution to its economic development and to achieve the Saudi 2030 vision.

1 Introduction

1.1 Introducing the Kingdom

The Kingdom of Saudi Arabia (henceforth KSA) is a country in the Middle East and located in the Southwest of Asia. It is expanded from the Red Sea in the west to the Arabian Gulf in the east. It is bordered by Jordan, Iraq, and Kuwait from the north, Yemen and Oman from the south, the Arabian Gulf, and the United Arab Emirates, Qatar, and Bahrain from the east, and the Red Sea in the west (Exhibit 1).

The capital city of the KSA is Riyadh. Exhibit 2 shows the modern development of the city attracting more inhabitants increasing in number from 150,000 inhabitants

---

W. J. Aloulou (✉) · R. Alshaeel
Imam Mohammad Ibn Saud Islamic University, Riyadh, Saudi Arabia
e-mail: Wjaloulou@imamu.edu.sa; raalshaeel@imamu.edu.sa

© The Author(s), under exclusive license to Springer Nature Switzerland AG 2023
V. Ramadani et al. (eds.), *Family Business in Gulf Cooperation Council Countries*, Contributions to Management Science,
https://doi.org/10.1007/978-3-031-17262-5_6

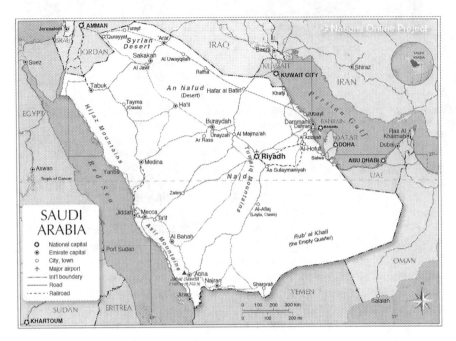

Exhibit 1 Political map of the KSA (Nations Online Project, 2020). *Note*: Everyone is free to use this map for educational purposes, referring to the Nations Online Project

to over 7 million people making it the most populous city in Saudi Arabia, third most populous in the Middle East, and 38th most populous in Asia (Aloulou & Arifi, 2022; rcrc.gov.sa; riyadh.sa). The city is expected to rise to 8.3 million by 2030.

1.2 Membership of the GCC

Saudi Arabia is also a member of the Gulf Cooperation Council that was founded on May 25, 1981. Among the members, the country shares common culture (Muslim and Arab heritage) and regulations in different fields helping them to promote and facilitate their integration since the establishment of the council (Ramady, 2010).

1.3 Flag and Emblem of KSA

The flag of KSA (Exhibit 3) is characterized by the following: A green field with the Shahada or Muslim creed was written in the Thuluth script in white above a horizontal sword, having its tip pointed to the left. Its emblem (or national symbols)

Family Business in Saudi Arabia   93

Exhibit 2 Night view of Riyadh city. *Source:* Pixabay (https://pixabay.com/photos/riyadh-saudi-arabia-city-night-2197496/). *Note:* Free for commercial use. No attribution required

Exhibit 3 Flag and emblem of Saudi Arabia

is characterized by the following: A palm green tree surmounting two swords in saltire argent hilted or in base.

1.4 Panorama of the KSA's Economy

Saudi Arabia is the largest economy in the Middle East and the richest Arab country in the region possessing around 17% of the world's proven petroleum reserves.

Since some years ago, the country has increased its rankings in different sectors. Its GDP is about US $700.12 Billion. However, its growth rate is about −4.1% in 2020, and certainly affected by the pandemic global crisis of COVID-19. In the first quarter of 2022, the Saudi economy grows by 9.9% on an annual basis achieving the highest growth rate since 2011. It is expected to grow 7% in 2022, ahead of other countries in the Gulf Cooperation Council, according to the Global Economic Update report by the World Bank. This growth is driven by continued growth in non-oil sectors, and this confirms the direction that the country is shown for the diversification of its economy.

In terms of the Human Development Index, the country ranks 40th (with an index of 0.854) globally among countries with very high human development. It achieved tenth place among the G20 countries (United Nations Development Programme, 2020). According to the World Bank Group's Doing Business 2020 report (World Bank, 2020), Saudi Arabia placed 62nd globally in ease of doing business rankings with an overall score of 71.6 out of 100. Saudi Arabia accelerated business climate reforms and joins ranks of top 10 global business climate improvers. These impressive reforms showed the real commitment of the country to fulfil the main pillar of the Saudi 2030 Vision: A thriving economy.

In 2020, the unemployment rate in Saudi Arabia was about 5.86%. It increased to 6.90% in the fourth quarter of 2021 from 6.60% in the third quarter of 2021 according to the General Authority for Statistics, GaStat.

Saudi Arabia has been ranked among the top 10 countries in the world in digital skills/capabilities, according to the IMD World Digital Competitiveness Index (2020) from the Global Competitiveness Report 2020 (IMD, 2021). The continuous leadership of the country is consolidated, and its permanent progress is preserved in various indicators. Saudi government is investing heavily in digital economy support and initiatives (recovery programs, SANID initiatives: POS end-to-end sales, e-commerce solutions, etc.) with the goal of enhancing value creation and national prosperity and reducing the impacts of the COVID-19 pandemic on SMEs and on private sector (Monstaa't, 2020; Arabian Business, 2020). The KSA's progress is attributed to four factors: adoption of information and communication technology, flexible work arrangements, the national digital skills, and the legal digital framework. This achievement is made possible through the readiness of the country to adopt digital transformation and innovation in the business environment.

Saudi Arabia's Economic Freedom score is 62.4, making its economy the 83rd freest in the 2020 Index. The country is ranked ninth among 14 countries in the MENA region, and its overall score is nearly equal to the regional and world averages. Its overall score has increased by 1.7 points due to higher property rights and judicial effectiveness scores. Given that the index of Economic Freedom is based on the rule of law, government size, regulatory efficiency, and open market dimensions.

According to the Global Gender Gap Report (World Economic Forum, 2020), Saudi Arabia is ranked 146th out of 153 countries for gender parity with a score of 0.599. Saudi women do not have equal rights to men in the Kingdom.

Table 1 Country profile

Total **land** area of the country [a]	2,149,690 km^2
Population (% Saudi) in 2022 [b]	35,906,829 (more than 69%)
Population yearly growth rate [b,f]	1.59% (1.63% 2022 Est.)
GDP 2020 US$ (Growth rate) [b]	700.12 billion (−4.1%)
GDP Q1/2022 Growth rate [a]	9.9%
Score in HDI index (and ranking) [d]	0.854 (40 / 189)
Ranking in "Ease of Doing Business" 2020 [b]	62nd / 190 (71.6 /10)
WEF Global Competitiveness 2020 [e]	36th /140 (70.0/100)
Ranking Digital competitiveness 2021 (score) [g]	36[h] / 64 (64.349 / 100)
Unemployment rate [i]	5.86%
Global Innovation Index 2021 [h]	66th / 132 (31.8 / 100)
Economic Freedom Rank and Index (2022) [j]	118th / 55.5 / 100
Global Gender Gap index 2021 [e]	147th / 156 (0.603 / 1)

Source: (a) General Authority for Statistics' official website, (b) www.worldometers.info (2022); (c) World Bank (2020), (d) UNDP (2020), (e) World Economic Forum (2020), (f) World Factbook (2022), (g) IMD Digital World Competitiveness ranking 2021, (h) Dutta et al., (2021), (i) Statistica (2020); (j) Heritage Foundation (2020)

Table 1 summarized all these indicators according to different official reports and international organizations.

1.5 Saudi 2030 Vision

The Kingdom of Saudi Arabia witnessed a significant transformation of its economy since the announcement of its Vision 2030 (Saudi Council of Economic and Development Affairs, 2016).

Three pillars are at the foundation of the Saudi Vision 2030:

- "A vibrant society" to promote the Saudi cultural heritage, the religious tourism, provide a healthy and balanced lifestyle, empower the society with the basic essentials of life, and build a health care system.
- "Thriving economy with rewarding opportunities and investment in the long term and open for business for leveraging the unique position of the KSA."
- "Ambitious nation effectively governed" to increase the KSA's ranking in the Government Effectiveness Index from 80 to 20 and to raise the E-Government Survey Index ranking from 36 to among the top five nations; and responsibly enabled to raise household savings from 6% to 10%, to raise the non-profit sector's contribution to the GDP from less than 1% to 5% and to rally one million volunteers per year.

Exhibit 4 Riyadh City by day; photo © 2022, by Riyadh Ashaeel

The KSA has reaffirmed its commitment to the 2030 agenda for sustainable development and the achievement of the SDGs and has made significant improvements in key aspects of human development and women empowerment in the workplace (Aloulou & Alarifi, 2022). The Saudi Vision 2030 has the ambition to transform the SME sector into an engine for economic growth with clearly defined priorities. This sector of SMEs has over 750,000 SMEs and is growing 15% in Q1 2020 as climate improves and SMEs amounted to 62% of all employment in the private sector, with each enterprise on average hiring 12 people (Monshaa't, 2022). This also can be explained by the change of mindset of Saudis to venture into new businesses. More than 31% of SMEs are located in Riyadh making the capital one of the most dynamic cities in Saudi Arabia for SMEs (Exhibit 4).

2 Business Ecosystem

2.1 An Ecosystem in a Constant Change

It was identified, before, that Saudi Arabia is transforming its economy and its business environment to promote entrepreneurship and innovation among all participants involved in its development (Aloulou, 2021, 2018a; Aloulou & Al-Othman, 2022). The country is establishing the necessary conditions to move toward a knowledge-based economy (Nurunnabi, 2017). The Saudi government has taken important measures to support entrepreneurship and innovation among people and organizations. The Saudi business ecosystem has grown significantly during the last decade in terms of programs, procedures, incentives, institutions, and supporting organizations (Aloulou & Al-Othman, 2022; Ashri, 2019). A series of reforms were led in relation to an improved investment climate and targeting high-tech entrepreneurship and main sectors (tourism, health, culture, entertainment, sports, etc.) (OC&C Strategy Consultants, 2018; Monshaa't, 2022).

It was shown that despite the backdrop of COVID-19, the country has attracted investors in many Saudi start-ups (mostly e-commerce) marking an important increase in total funding through venture capital (MAGNITT, 2020). New legislation is done for starting new businesses, supporting and protecting investors (business angels, venture capital, etc.), and improving the status of foreign investors. The last official report "ease of doing business" by World bank proves such facts (World Bank, 2020).

Many initiatives at the heart of the Saudi 2030 Vision are being launched in Saudi Arabia to provide business opportunities to private sector and quality job opportunities for the next generation:

- Saudi Green Initiative toward a sustainable future to reduce carbon emissions, planting trees, and protecting land and sea.[1]
- The implementation of large-scale and major infrastructure projects, new megacities planned, and mega development in Riyadh city based on public–private partnerships (Al Ula masterplan, NEOM, TROJENA, OXAGON, THE LINE, Diriyah Gate, Qiddiyah, etc.) announced as a Saudi Arabia's USD 900BN development plan.[2]
- Vision realization programs: Public investment fund program, housing program, pilgrim experience program, fiscal sustainability program, human capability development program, quality of life program, national transformation program, privatization program, health sector transformation program, financial sector development program, national industrial development, and logistics program (Exhibit 5).

---

[1] https://www.saudigreeninitiative.org/

[2] https://www.thebig5saudi.com/wp-content/uploads/sites/6/2021/03/Saudi-Arabia-USD-900bn-development-plan.pdf

Exhibit 5 Water Tower in Al Khobar, Al-Sharqiyyah province; photo © 2022, Riyadh Ahshaeel

2.2 Saudi Entrepreneurship Context

The latest report of GEM (2022) considered the Saudi environment for entrepreneurship as the most supportive environment after seeking the point of view of

Family Business in Saudi Arabia   99

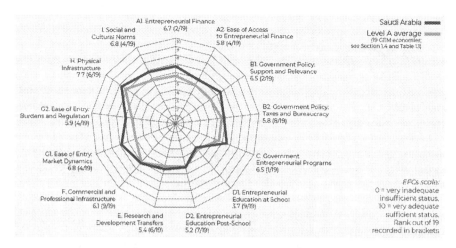

Exhibit 6 Expert ratings of the entrepreneurial framework conditions. Source: GEM (2022)

national experts on main framework conditions (e.g., entrepreneurial finance, government policy, government entrepreneurial programs, entrepreneurial education, research and development transfers, commercial and professional infrastructure, easy of entry, physical infrastructure, and social and cultural norms). The country has the highest National Entrepreneurship Context Index of 6.1 out of 10 after, respectively, UAE, the Netherlands, and Finland. The UAE, as a member of the GCC, is the only economy to have scored as sufficient or better for all framework conditions (6.8 out of 10) (Exhibit 6).

2.3 Conduciveness of the Environment for Entrepreneurship Amidst COVID-19 Pandemic

Despite the enduring of COVID-19 pandemic in 2020 and 2021, more than 80% of the adult population in Saudi Arabia perceived good opportunities to start a business. Many of them see new opportunities caused by the pandemic and its implications. In 6 of the 43 participating economies, more than 3 out of 4 adults agree or strongly agree that it is easy to start a business in that country, peaking at more than 9 out of 10 in Saudi Arabia (GEM, 2021). According to the GEM report (2021), Saudi Arabia recorded the highest assessment of responses (of entrepreneurs and of government) to the pandemic, respectively, 7.7 and 8.4 out of 10. It ranked first worldwide in responding to the pandemic.

For the country, the different achievements were made thanks to business environment characterized by flexibility and the ability to face challenges and due to the essential reforms in the entrepreneurship environment to business start-up procedures.

3 Family Business

3.1 Introductory Aspects

Saudi Arabia is one of the most prominent countries in the GCC region. Moreover, Saudi family businesses are a cornerstone of the Middle East's and GCC's economies and they are growing during the last decades (Ramady & Sohail, 2010; Aloulou, 2018b). In 2007, the number of Saudi family firms was about 621,400 companies (Al-Dubai et al., 2012). In 2009, the total number of businesses operating in Saudi Arabia reached the figure of 763,589, and most of them are family-owned business representing around 95% (Alshaeel, 2016).

The most recent statistics showed that Saudi Arabia had approximately one million establishments in 2017 (Statistica.com). Furthermore, according to the Family Governance Forum and a study conducted by the National Center of Family Business (CNFB) by the end of 2017 and in early 2018, 538,000 family businesses in the Kingdom were estimated to exist, representing about 63% of the total operating enterprises. They contributed $216 billion to the GDP of the country, and had employed about 7.2 million people, representing 52% of the total workforce (Alsharif, 2019). These statistics prove how important are family businesses in the Saudi economy. In the GEM report of 2018, Saiz-Alvarez et al. (2022) highlighted the prevalence of family businesses in Saudi Arabia over the entire population of the study. There are significant percentages of individuals involved in the ownership and management of family businesses.

3.2 Saudi Family Business Ecosystem

Regarding the most important actors relevant to the family business in Saudi Arabia, institutions, organizations, and networks are providing their services to family businesses.

Mapping the Saudi family business ecosystem necessitates to consider the environment of family businesses at three levels: micro, meso, and macro levels. At the micro-level, family businesses are directly influenced by the family itself, the nature of ownership (founder-s, family members, etc.), and the nature of the business itself. At the meso-level, family businesses maintain a direct relationship with its customers, partners, and direct suppliers. At the macro-level, family businesses consider the role of the main actors at the national and GCC levels. These actors in the family business ecosystem concern with the following:

- At the national level:
  - Ministries (Ministry of Commerce; Ministry of Investment, Ministry of Human resources and social development, etc.) as government institutions.
  - National Center of Family Businesses (NCFB).

Family Business in Saudi Arabia

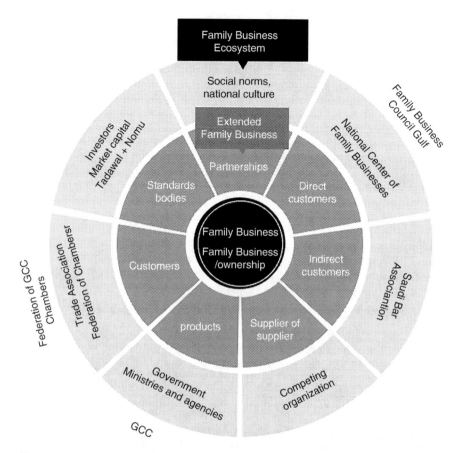

Exhibit 7 Saudi Family business Ecosystem. Source: Authors' elaboration

- Trade associations, Federation of national chambers, etc.
- Capital Market Authority (CMA), Saudi Stock Exchange (Tadawul), and Nomu Parallel Market as partners to transform family businesses into joint-stock companies by going public and gaining visibility in the market.
- Saudi Bar Association and Saudi Center for Commercial Arbitration as professional bodies for solving family disputes involving inheritance, etc.
- Advisory firms for family businesses (Business Family House as an example), etc.

• At the GCC region:

- GCC council as a political and economic alliance providing support.
- Federation of GCC chambers, considered among the most important institutional frameworks that support the private sector in GCC countries (Exhibit 7).

Exhibit 8 Logo of the National Center for Family Businesses

3.3 The National Center for Family Businesses

Started in October 2012, the National Center for Family Businesses (NCFB) [3] aims to help in:

- Sustaining the development of family businesses.
- Consolidating the concept of governance.
- Encouraging them to invest in the capital market.
- Solving problems and conflicts that may arise in such companies (Exhibit 8).

The center plays a key role in coordinating with the Ministry of Commerce officials to share the views of family businesses and their board members on the new Companies Law. The new Companies Law supports the sustainability and growth of family businesses through governance and the family charter, currently used in dispute settlements. This charter is also deemed as part of Companies Law and allows partners to refer to it and add it to the family business agreements. A new Companies Law issued on June 28, 2022, addresses all challenges facing family businesses in Saudi Arabia. It will enable concluding of a family charter that regulates family ownership in the family business, its governance and management, work policy, employment of family members, and distribution of profits so as to ensure the sustainability of these companies (Saudi Gazette, 2022).

3.4 Main Facts of the Contribution of Family Businesses to the Economy

The investments of family businesses in the Kingdom exceeded $66 billion in 2014. A recent study conducted in 2018 (National Center for Family Businesses, NCFB) revealed that family businesses in the Kingdom represent 63% of the private sector

---

[3] https://ncfb.org.sa/

entities in Saudi Arabia, and account for 66% of the private sector gross domestic product (GDP). Ninety-two percent of the family businesses are located in major areas of the country with 45% in Riyadh, 28% in Makkah, and 18% in the Eastern Province. The largest percentage of Saudi family companies fall under the legal form of limited liability company, as they are more in line with the reality and composition of Saudi families.

Family businesses contribute more than 800 billion riyals ($213.3 billion) or 32 percent annually to the Kingdom's domestic income and provide many job opportunities for citizens. For instance, the family business sector is vital and plays a prominent role in the development of the national economy in addition to its distinction in the process of localizing national talents of both sexes (Saudi Gazette, 2018). More than 80% of the total workers in the private sector work in family businesses, which stresses the need to strengthen and build the capabilities of family businesses and increase their adaptation to the new economic environment imposed by "Vision 2030" and to benefit from the promising investment opportunities generated by it.

3.5 *Importance and Main Characteristics of Saudi Family Businesses*

In Saudi Arabia, the family is the most important social institution and the Islamic values are found in business relationships with family members to an extent that family is in the business and business is in the family (Pistrui & Fahed-Sreih, 2017). In the same line, Ramady & Sohail (2010) identified a model depicting the major forces influencing family business in Saudi Arabia: cultural forces; Hereditary forces; Family relationships; Religion; Social class, and other group membership forces. Arabian culture is based on ethics, generosity, respect, and solidarity. These cultural values and forces affect the way the family businesses are managed, and decision-making is processed. Also, Islam religion governs every aspect of Muslim life including family business conduct.

Alrubaishi et al. (2021) revealed the importance of family ties (relations between family members at work or between incumbent and successor; communication, family bond/cohesion, family structure, etc.) and culture (Islamic values, kinship ties, family structure, preservation of goods manners) in the entrepreneurial and organizational behavior of family firms in general and the influence of Islamic capital on the intergenerational transfer of family legacy in particular. Similarly, Balila (2020) argued that social ties (family kinship and friendship from the same tribes) are still valued and have their influence on operating businesses.

3.6 Focusing on Saudi Arabian Culture

Saudi Arabia's culture is a unique fusion of Islam and Arab customs. Saudi Arabia recognizes Islam as its official religion. Religion is one of the most important and distinctive features of Arab culture. Numerous researchers have identified religion as a primary factor that affects the majority of elements of Arab culture (Shahin & Wright, 2004; Kalliny & Gentry, 2007). It is the aspect that has the greatest impact on culture in Islamic countries, particularly in Arab ones. Islam, a whole way of life, is the foundation of Arabic culture, including its language, social structure, and traditions (Kavoossi, 2000). According to Al-Shaikh, the political and economic structures combine elements of socialism, capitalism, and secularism. The argument that Arab culture has been influenced by globalization and, specifically, Western behavior, supports this. Nevertheless, Islam is the most dominant religion in Arab countries and consolidates several attributes of Arab culture such as honesty, loyalty, and trust (Ali, 1995, Al-Shaikh, 2003). Saudi Arabian culture is influenced by the mixture of Islam and politics, most decisions, especially those involving business, are made as a result of Islam (Elamin & Alomaim, 2011). Furthermore, the social interactions that take place between members of the family and society to establish the conventions and practices that makeup Saudi Arabia's organizational culture. Ownership of a business in Saudi Arabia enables a family to rise to a distinguished level in terms of social influence by improving its financial situation (Davis et al., 2000).

The principles of Islam guide the performance of the people and forms a solid consistent culture that includes the entire society (Alanazi & Rodrigues, 2003; Baker et al., 2011). Additionally, the cultural research conducted by Hofstede (1991, cited by Branine, 2011) showed Arab culture to have a high-power distance, high uncertainty avoidance, to be strong in terms of collectivism, masculinity, and to have a short time orientation (Branine, 2011). Moreover, the family businesses in Saudi Arabia are powerfully influenced by the Saudi context, including culture, Islamic ethics, and values (Alshaeel, 2016).

Hofstede (2001) stated that there is a clear relationship between power distance and authoritarianism. In the power distance dimension, choices are made based on preferences to subordinates and loyalty to superiors, not based on excellence. Countries with a large power distance, where inequality is understood, highlight a dependency relationship between directors and assistants (Hofstede, 2001). Such as the Arab countries which scored 80 out of 104; they were ranked seventh among the 50 countries included in the study. In contrast, cultures with lower power distance such as Austria are described by agreement between directors and assistants to minimize inequality (Obeidat et al., 2012).

Several studies (Mellahi, 2007; Branine, 2011) show that the Arab world and GCC countries, particularly Saudi Arabia, have a large power distance, that is because, the leaders, the wealthy, the religious, the educated, and the elderly, have higher positions, authority, and income that followers do not have, although the different relationships of people with each other give different levels of power distance in practice perspective.

Bjerke & Al-Meer (1993) found that Saudi directors scored high on power distance, suggesting that there is a social distance between directors and subordinates regarding authority. Moreover, Saudi directors also seem to have a high uncertainty avoidance orientation and prefer a close social context in both organizational and institutional lives (Bjerke & Al-Meer, 1993). Consequently, they are mostly categorized as risk avoiders, therefore vital decisions are frequently made at the highest level of management.

3.7 Islamic Inheritance Law and Family Firm Succession

Inheritance is a common concept present in all religions and has been around since the earliest human societies, but it has different forms and applications. Inheritance law in the Islamic religion has great significance because it regulates the financial rights of the heirs. In Muslim Arab cultures, the law of succession stipulates that every single person receives the same share. Nevertheless, the distribution of inheritance and succession are important topics but hardly any studies about them are found (Palliam et al., 2011).

Islamic Inheritance Laws were obtained from the holy book (Quran). Islamic inheritance law manages the laws and rules to divide inheritance among all successors, with the intention to act justly to all levels of successors and to avoid differences between them (Awang, 2008). The method of distribution is called (faraid) which is founded on the verses of inheritance in Surah al-Nisa (Chapter "*Family Business in Qatar*"; Verses 11, 12, and 176) of the Holy Quran and the Prophetic traditions. A number of people have the right to particular shares of a deceased's estate under the scheme of faraid. However, these people are categorized into two categories. The first comprises the Quranic heirs (primary), as they are stated in the Quran, with certain portions. The second category includes residuary heirs (secondary), who might be qualified for either the entire estate or the balance of it, according to specific circumstances (Awang, 2008). Moreover, after all debts and liabilities of the deceased have been paid, the remainder of his/her estate will be distributed according to the rules of Islamic law calculations faraid (Bulbul, 2013) (Exhibit 9).

The family business has a special structure, as it is a mixture of elements of the individual relationship, the control of the company, and ownership that mainly assurances the business to continue under the family name (Sharma, 2004; Longenecker et al., 2006). The succession plan is one of the approaches that can be arranged to keep the ownership of the company under the control of the family, by formulating and transferring company control to the family members as successors to satisfy the family interests (Carrigan & Buckley, 2008; Yu et al., 2012). However, the inheritance law plays an important role in that it allows the family to preserve control of the business, specifying the rights of family members in the deceased's

Exhibit 9 Makkah al-Mukarramah, Clock Royal Tower (left) and Al Masjid Al Haram (right); photo © 2022, Riyadh Alshaeel

estate even with the lack of a succession plan. The teachings of inheritance law explicitly indicate that only persons related by blood or family members will have rights in the deceased's estate (Bulbul, 2013). In contrast, the family business might be dismantled if the family members that inherited shares have no intention to keep it and reject taking leadership of the company, which might result in the shares being sold off to outsiders.

3.8 Main Key Factors of Success

There are various factors for the success of family businesses in Saudi Arabia which can be like other family businesses over all the world (Chamber, 2013). These factors include, firstly the importance of the early preparations of a plan for the next generation (Sharma, 2004). Secondly, the separation of the ownership and management of the company. Thirdly, the attraction of talented non-family individuals to work in the enterprise (Poutziouris et al., 2006). Fourth, the importance of researching successful businesses and imitating them in order to learn from their experience and prevent failure-causing elements. Fifth, the importance of the commitment to ethical values and Islamic morals and legitimacy and the role of philanthropic and charitable endowments for the continuation of Saudi family businesses across generations which reflect both the company and the family (Alshaeel, 2016).

3.9 Successful Saudi Family Businesses

The Kingdom of Saudi Arabia includes a distinguished group of successful family businesses, which operate in different sectors and represent one of the most important pillars of the Saudi economy.

Saudi companies dominate the list of Top 100 Arab Family Businesses made by Forbes in the Middle East in 2021, with 36 from Saudi Arabia. They reflect a form of a successful partnership between FAMILY and BUSINESS.

Table 2 presents the main facts of the most important Saudi family businesses in terms of rankings, name of the company, establishment and leadership, and quick facts about the starting up, investment the company holds, and sectors in focus. These successful businesses are listed as follows:

1. Olayan Group as the strongest among Saudi family businesses.
2. Al Muhaidib Group as the most important diversified investment conglomerate in the region.
3. Rashed Abdul Rahman Al Rashed & Sons Group as one of the largest private sector investors in the Saudi Stock market.
4. Abdul Latif Jameel as one of the largest distributors of Toyota cars around the world.
5. Assila Investments Holding is among the largest individual investors in Saudi.
6. Al Nahla Group as one of the oldest businesses in Saudi Arabia and belongs to the Sharbatly family.
7. E. A. Juffali & Brothers as Saudi Arabia's largest private enterprise and among industry pioneers in the country.
8. Yousuf M.A. Naghi & Sons Group, a diversified Jeddah-based firm and one of the well-known conglomerates in Saudi Arabia.
9. Zamil Group Holding, a Saudi family-owned global company with diversified industrial operations and capabilities, commercial interests, and alliances with leading international organizations.
10. Saudi FAS Holding as the largest franchise retailer in KSA and the MENA region.

In a recent report from Family Capital (2020a), most of these successful Saudi family businesses were also present in the Middle East Top 150. They counted 54 companies out of 150. However, in the Family Capital report (2020a), only three of them have their impact globally (Olayan Group; Al Rashed & Sons Group; Abdul Latif Jameel). From a regional perspective, European family businesses make up the big share of 750 companies before Asia-Pacific and North America. However, from

Table 2 Forbes Middle East: Saudi top 10 family businesses in 2021

Rank (national)	Rank	Company	Establishment and leadership (Chairperson)	Quick facts
1.	1	Olayan Group	1947, Hutham Olayan	– First founded by Suliman Olayan as a contracting and trading company in Saudi Arabia. The group has a diversified portfolio. – The family holds shares in many companies (Credit Suisse, Saudi British Bank, etc.). – In Saudi Arabia, the group bottles Coca-Cola, runs Burger King restaurants, and manufactures cans and paper.
2.	6	Al Muhaidib Group	1943, Sulaiman Al Muhaidib	– Founded as a small trading business. – The group today has over 200 companies across different sectors. – The family holds shares in many companies (Savola Group, Bawan Holding Company, Middle East Paper Company, and Al Yamamah Steel Industries. – Sulaiman Al Muhaidib is chairman of the Al Muhaidib Group, the Savola Group, and the Rafal Real Estate Development Company. – In January 2021, the Al Muhaidib Social Foundation won the King Abdulaziz Quality Award for the charitable sector.
3.	7	Rashed Abdul Rahman Al Rashed & Sons Group	1950, Abdulaziz Al Rashed	– Founded more than seven decades ago by Rashed Al Rashed. – The group today owns 26 companies that employ a total of more than 13,000 people and that operate in many sectors. – The company's investments include banks (Banque Saudi Fransi, Arab National Bank) and steel industries (Al Yamamah Steel Industries) making it one of the biggest private investors in the Saudi Stock market – The family also has investments in the Egyptian stock exchange.
4.	8	Abdul Latif Jameel	1945, Mohammed Abdul Latif Jameel	– Abdul Latif Jameel was founded in Jeddah by Abdul Latif Jameel as a small trading business in 1945. – Today, it is present in more than

(continued)

Table 2 (continued)

Rank (national)	Rank	Company	Establishment and leadership (Chairperson)	Quick facts
				30 countries over six continents and employs 11,000 people. – JIMCO, the global investment arm of the Jameel family, was one of the early investors in electric and utility-scale solar power projects outside the country.
5.	9	Assila Investments	2010, Abdullah Mohammed Al-Issa	– Mohammed Al-Issa and Sons Holding was founded by Mohammed Al-Issa in 1970 and became Assila Investments in 2010. – Al-Issa was one of the largest individual investors in the Saudi Stock Market (Investments in Tadawul are worth $2.7 billion, owning shares in Riyad Bank, Savola, Dur Hospitality, Taiba Investments).
6.	14	Al Nahla Group	1996, Abdulrahman Hassan Sharbatly	– The Al Nahla Group was established by the late Hasan Abbas Sharbatly, who previously founded Riyad Bank. Today the group owns 8.7% of Riyad Bank, worth $1.7 billion as of April 2021. The holding company focuses on the automotive (Audi, Porsche, Ferrari, and Maserati), real estate (City Stars Mall in Egypt), trading, and investment sectors with a focus on Saudi Arabia, the Gulf, Egypt, and across various industrial sectors.
7.	15	E. A. Juffali & Brothers	1946, Khaled Al Juffali	– Established as an electric power, cement, and communications business. – The company is now a diversified group operating across numerous sectors including automotive, technology, and construction. – Juffali's international partnerships include brands such as IBM, Mercedes-Benz, Siemens, Carrier, and Michelin. – The company currently employs more than 7000 people and owns 5% of Wataniya Insurance.

(continued)

Table 2 (continued)

Rank (national)	Rank	Company	Establishment and leadership (Chairperson)	Quick facts
				– The family also owns a significant stake in National Automobile Industry (joint venture with Mercedes-Benz Commercial Vehicles to assemble Mercedes-Benz Commercial vehicles locally).
8.	16	Yousuf M.A. Naghi & Sons Group	1911, Mohammed Yousuf Naghi	– The group has a diversified portfolio of four companies managed by the four sons (each manages a company). – The group is Saudi Arabia's exclusive sales and distribution agent for Rolls-Royce, BMW, Mini, and Jaguar and operates and manages one of the largest bus and coach companies in the Middle East with over 12,000 units. – The group operated in the FMCG sector.
9.	19	Zamil Group Holding	1920, Khalid A. Al-Zamil	– Through its 14 wholly owned companies and 12 joint ventures, Zamil Group Holding operates across several sectors (building materials, manufacturing, offshore, petrochemicals, trade and services, real estate… – The family firm has a workforce of 12,000 people. – The Zamil Industrial Investment Company and Sahara International Petrochemical Company (SIPCHEM) are two publicly listed companies on the Saudi Stock Exchange (Tadawul).
10.	20	Saudi FAS Holding	1975, Fawaz Al Hokair	– Saudi FAS Holding is the holding company of the Al Hokair family and is equally owned by brothers Fawaz, Salman, and Abdul Majeed. – The family is the largest shareholder in the Fawaz Abdulaziz Alhokair Co. – The holding has interests in fashion retail and electronics and operates in 16 countries across the Middle East, Europe, and the United States and employs around 15,000 people.

(continued)

Family Business in Saudi Arabia   111

Table 2 (continued)

Rank (national)	Rank	Company	Establishment and leadership (Chairperson)	Quick facts
				– It owns 65% of Arabian Centers, the largest mall operator in the kingdom.
The rest of Saudi companies in the list of top 100 in the Middle East				Sedco Holding (21); Dallah Albaraka Holding (22); BinDawood Group (28); Saudi Bugshan Group (29); Zahid Group (31); Ajlan & Bros Group (34); MASIC (37); Bait Al-Batterjee Group (39); Aujan Group Holding (41); Nesma Holding Group (42); Xenel (44); Omar Kassem Alesayi Group (45); Obeikan Investment Group (48); Abdullah Al Othaim Holding (50); Arabian Fal Holding (56); AlOthman Holding (57); Abunayyan Holding (58); Tamer Group (62); Almajdouie Group (66); Naif Alrajhi Investment (67); Sumou Holding (68); Alkhorayef Group (70); Al Faisaliah Group (74); Al Qahtani Holding (76); Alturki Holding (88); Tamimi group (99)
36% of the listed companies un the Top 100 are Saudi				

Source: Forbes (2021)

a country perspective, the US remains the dominant center for the world of family businesses with 166 out of 750 companies (Family Capital, 2020b).

3.10 Challenges of Saudi Family Businesses

3.10.1 Common Challenges

How to manage the paradox of the desire to maintain and respect tradition and family values whilst thriving to adapt and progress in response to a rapidly changing economic and business environment? And how to make the transition from the one generation to the next?

These are the important challenging questions that any family business asks and try to respond to them (PwC Middle East, 2021; Deloitte, 2016).

In 2013, the Ministry of Commerce and Investment has issued the first version of a guiding charter for the Saudi family businesses, aiming at enhancing the family's business values, achieving the objectives of the companies, and developing their business according to an institutional framework that supports the possibility of their expansion, and increases the chances of their success (Ministry of Commerce and Industry, 2013; Chehab, 2018). In 2018, this guiding charter was adopted for the family businesses to regulate the family property in the company, the relations and the transfer ownership among the family members, and the criteria of their employment. With such charter, the family members will be aware of their rights and obligations, balancing the interests of the family members and the company's interests. Furthermore, the charter sets out the rules for dispute settlement that may be encountered. It also aims at maximizing the value of the company. With this guiding charter, Saudi Arabia's family-owned businesses get new corporate governance guidelines.

The most important features of the Guiding Charter are:

- Organizing the work and defining the role of the family members in the executive system of the family company and how the tasks are to be carried out.
- Determining the profit distribution policy of the family company.
- Drawing up the mechanisms of trading family shares in a manner that prevents the transfer of ownership to a party that does not belong to the family.
- Organizing the method of resolving conflicts that may arise between family members (terms of employment for anyone who belongs to the family).

As commented by Saudi scholars (Alkahtani, 2021; Alsabt, 2018; Alshaeel, 2016), the charter handled many details that represent a major challenge for family businesses in Saudi Arabia, and organized them in a precise manner: organizational structure of the family firm; its constitution and institution (family council; board of directors structure and its members; shares; disclosure and transparency).

While talking about the vital role that family businesses play, not only at the economic level, but also at the social level, we cannot lose sight of the obstacles that surround them. Some of them come from the family itself, and some of them are caused by the internal/external environment. This constitutes a major challenge for these businesses to deal with quickly, and find radical solutions to it, to be able to continue and progress. In reviewing previous studies on Saudi family businesses (Alkahtani, 2021, 2017; Alsabt, 2018; Alshaeel, 2016; AlRebdi & Mohamad, 2021; Ekanem & Alrossais, 2017; Sfakianakis, 2009), several issues of concern to and challenges for Saudi family businesses are related to:

- Disputes over management between generations to whom ownership passes after the first generation without a clear succession planning.
- Disputes related to the sale of shares, and the refusal to transfer the ownership of the company to parties outside the family.

- Conflicts within the family itself, which are deeply reflected in family business disrupting the course of its development.
- Conflicts over the division of inheritance in the second and third generations.
- The unwillingness of the new generations to enter the same field, and their tendency to work for other institutions and or in other sectors.
- Intertwined powers, and strong confusion between the company's possession and its management.
- Failure to apply governance and a belief that it is not useful because of the idea that the owners are keen to maintain their dominance over the company.
- The company floundered after the death of its founders and the lack of readiness of the successors.
- The inability of the company to keep pace with continuous developments in the field of business.
- Working without clear and defined strategies and vision.
- The old generation rejected any sign of development or change, underestimated the capabilities and ideas of new generations, and did not accept risks.
- Absence of rigorous treatment when dealing with expenses and profits.
- The lack of a strong and integrated reference for financial and administrative information.
- Being present in an uncertain and unstable environment and may increase the risk of economic crises.

3.10.2 COVID-19 Challenge and Family Business Resilience

The PwC report (PwC Middle East, 2021) clearly illustrated the resilience and agility of 73 family businesses in the Middle East. The report showed their optimism about the perspectives of growth in the coming few years and their digital capability to emerge stronger from the pandemic. Some family businesses are repurposing their operations and diversifying their portfolios and expanding in new markets. They are also prioritizing (digital) transformation and accelerating it by shifting to digital services and work-from-home models. They are looking forward the future to prioritize sustainability goals (engaging in social responsibility activities, sustainable business practices) and professionalize family governance. Family businesses demonstrated resilience amid COVID-19 and are prepared to lead the post-pandemic recovery. According to a KPMG (2021) report, Saudi-based CEOs sought to strengthen digital resilience, taped disruptive technologies, and made aggressive digital investment strategies. Many organizations have coped well with the COVID-19 pandemic, showing resilience as they dealt with notable change, uncertainty, and disruption.

3.11 Women and Saudi Family Businesses: Leveraging an Untapped Potential of Women

Similar to Strategy& (2014), KPMG (2022) published a study surveying the opinions of Saudi women in family businesses in Saudi Arabia. Insights gathered from interviewing women business leaders working in family businesses were shaped into four themes:

- Varying roles of women in family business and the gender differences that women face in relation to treatment and opportunities within the family business as well as the role of mentors play in advancing women within the family business.
- Leadership style differences between men and women in terms of personal characteristics (emotions, aggressiveness, etc.), but also under the influence of outdated stereotypes hindering women in the workplace in male-dominated sectors and industries.
- Primogeniture succession approach is followed as an implicit rule and a norm for Saudi family business for generations. Though primogeniture to sons is still present in Saudi Arabia, some of the Kingdom's most successful family businesses are opening up leadership opportunities for women and are addressing succession in a meritocratic way.
- Unique opportunities and mandatory legislation that affects women's opportunities within the business by using quotas for female representation at the management/board level or in the workplace. The government's support for women at work has transformed the landscape of the public and private sectors to employ them.

The role of women in the workplace and in family businesses is flourishing because of the changing social norms in the country and their profound effect on life and on family businesses. Saudi women are well educated, and they are mentored and empowered by either men or women. These recent social changes have increased the involvement of women in the workplace and in family businesses.

4 Concluding Remarks

This chapter described the family business phenomenon in Saudi Arabia. First, the chapter introduced the Saudi Arabia Country geographically and economically by providing insights into main potential of the country, its performance indicators, and the potential of family business sector. It also showcased the Saudi business ecosystem as being in constant evolution and as offering a conducive entrepreneurial context for businesses and entrepreneurs, even in case of COVID-19 pandemic. The chapter continued the presentation of the Saudi family business ecosystem and its components. Second, the chapter particularly focused on Saudi family businesses as key contributors to the Saudi economy and on their main characteristics and specificities according to Saudi culture and inheritance law, and the key factors of success of most important businesses according to recent rankings. Third, the chapter looked at the main challenges faced by family businesses such as corporate governance, board operations, succession planning and sustainability, and women's participation. COVID-19 is still another challenge for Saudi family businesses that can be overcome. The pandemic was considered as an external enabler and an opportunity for them to build their resilience for the future and the resilience of their leadership (Aloulou, 2022; Orient Planet Group, 2020).

The rapidly changing state of the world has served as a wake-up call for family business leaders looking toward the future of their firms (PwC Middle East, 2021; KPMG, 2021) and for family business scholars toward the future of research (Krueger et al., 2021).

References

Alanazi, F. M., & Rodrigues, A. (2003). Power bases and attribution in three cultures. *The Journal of Social Psychology, 143*, 375–395.

Al-Dubai, S. A. A., Ismail, K. N. I. K., & Amran, N. A. (2012). Overview of family business in Saudi Arabia. In *International conference on contemporary business and management* (pp. 367–376).

Alkahtani, A. W. (2021). Family-owned businesses in Saudi Arabia: Challenges and solutions from a legal perspective. *Int. J. Contemp. Manag. Inf. Technol, 1*(2), 16–22.

Aloulou, W. J. (2022). *Handbook of research on entrepreneurship and organizational resilience during unprecedented times*. IGI Global Publishing. Available at: https://www.igi-global.com/book/handbook-research-entrepreneurship-organizational-resilience/290551

Aloulou, W. J. (2021). Mapping incubation mechanisms in Saudi Arabia: State-of-the-art and challenges for the future. In S. Mian, M. Klofsten, & W. Lamine (Eds.), *International handbook of research on business and technology incubation and acceleration* (pp. 351–366). Edward Elgar Publisher. https://doi.org/10.4337/9781788974783.00029

Aloulou, W. J. (2018a). Enhancing Women's economic empowerment through entrepreneurship in Saudi Arabia. In E. Al-A'ali, M. Al-Shammari, & H. Masri (Eds.), *Arab women and their evolving roles in the global business landscape* (pp. 120–151). IGI Global. https://doi.org/10.4018/978-1-5225-3710-6.ch006

Aloulou, W. J. (2018b). Examining entrepreneurial orientation' dimensions–performance relationship in Saudi family businesses: Contingency role of family involvement in management. *Journal of Business Family Management, 8*(2), 126–145. https://doi.org/10.1108/JFBM-02-2018-0007

Aloulou, W. J., & Al-Othman, N. (2022). Entrepreneurship in Saudi Arabia. In L.-P. Dana, V. Ramadani, & R. Palalic (Eds.), *Entrepreneurship in GCC*. World Scientific Publishing. https://doi.org/10.1142/12082

Aloulou, W. J., & Alarifi, M. (2022). The context of business in Saudi Arabia. In L.-P. Dana, V. Salamzadeh Ramadani, & R. Palalic (Eds.), *Understanding contexts of business in Western Asia. Land of bazaars and high-tech booms* (pp. 477–494). World Scientific. https://doi.org/10.1142/9789811229695_0022

AlRebdi, A., & Mohamad, K. A. (2021). Unsustainable family business in Saudi Arabia-the roadmap ahead. *International Journal of Business and Management Research, 9*(2), 233–243.

Alrubaishi, D. (2017). Succession planning in family SMEs in Saudi Arabia: A descriptive study. In S. Basly (Ed.), *Family businesses in the Arab world* (pp. 223–245). Springer.

Alrubaishi, D., McAdam, M., & Harrison, R. (2021). Culture, Islamic capital, and the entrepreneurial behaviour of family firms in Saudi Arabia. *International Journal of Entrepreneurial Behavior & Research*.

Alsabt, H. A. (2018). *Planning to preserve Saudi Arabian family-owned companies for future generations: What we can learn from corporate governance Laws and Practices in the US and the UK*, Doctoral dissertation, Georgetown University Law Center. Available at: https://repository.library.georgetown.edu/bitstream/handle/10822/1062997/alsabt_hisham_ali_dissertation.pdf?sequence=1

Alshaeel, R. (2016, May). *A study of the factors influencing the laws and management of family business succession in Saudi Arabia*, Doctoral Thesis, Dundee Business School, Abertay University. Available online: https://rke.abertay.ac.uk/en/studentTheses/a-study-of-the-factors-influencing-the-laws-and-management-of-fam

Alsharif, D. T. (2019). *In Saudi Arabia, business runs in the family*. Available online at: https://www.arabnews.com/node/1579676.

Al-Shaikh, F. N. (2003). The practical reality theory and business ethics in non-Western context: Evidence from Jordan. *Journal of Management Development, 22*, 679–693.

Ali, A. J. (1995). Cultural discontinuity and Arab management thought. *International Studies of Management and Organization, 7*–30.

Arabian Business. (2020), "Saudi government to cover 60% of private sector salaries hit by COVID-19". *Arabian business*. Available at: https://www.arabianbusiness.com/banking-finance/444303-saudi-government-tocover-60-of-private-sector-salaries-hit-by-covid-19

Ashri, O.M. (2019). *On the fast track: Saudi Arabia's entrepreneurship ecosystem*. Accessed Sep 23, 2019, from https://www.entrepreneur.com/article/336766

Awang, M. R. (2008). The Islamic inheritance law (Faraid): The manifestation of compressive inheritance Management in Islam, *working paper* presented at the National Convention of Faraid and Hibah 2008, organised by the Islamic development Malaysia department (JAKIM) at the multipurpose hall of the Federal Territory Mosque.

Baker, E. W., Al-Gahtani, S., & Hubona, G. S. (2011). Cultural impacts on acceptance and adoption of information technology in a developing country. In *International comparisons of information communication technologies: Advancing applications: Advancing applications* (Vol. 54).

Balila, S., (2020). *Family business in Saudi Arabia*, Doctoral thesis, Newcastle University Business School. Available at: https://theses.ncl.ac.uk/jspui/bitstream/10443/4920/1/Balila%20S%202020.pdf

Branine, M. (2011). *Managing across cultures: Concepts, policies and practices*. Sage Publications Ltd.

Bjerke, B., & Al-Meer, A. (1993). Culture's consequences: management in Saudi Arabia. *Leadership and Organization Development Journal, 14*, 30–35.

Bulbul, A. (2013). Implication of Islamic law of inheritance: Ultimate solution to family conflict. *Asian Journal Of Applied Science And Engineering, 2*, 217–224.

Carrigan, M., & Buckley, J. (2008). 'What's so special about family business?'an exploratory study of UK and Irish consumer experiences of family businesses. *International Journal of Consumer Studies, 32*, 656–666.

Chehab, M. (2018). *Guiding charter for family-owned businesses in Saudi Arabia*. Altamimi & Co. Available at: https://www.tamimi.com/law-update-articles/guiding-charter-for-family-owned-businesses-in-saudi-arabia/

Chamber, A. (2013). *Saudi Family Business success*. Family Saudi Arabia: Asharqia Chamber.

Davis, J. A., Pitts, E. L., & Cormier, K. (2000). Challenges facing family companies in the Gulf region. *Family Business Review, 13*, 217–238.

Deloitte, (2016, May). *Next-generation family businesses. Evolution keeping family values alive*. Available at: https://www2.deloitte.com/content/dam/Deloitte/global/Documents/Strategy/gx-family-business-nextgen-survey.pdf

Dutta, S., Lanvin, B., Leon, L.R., & Wunsch-Vincent, S. (2021). *Global innovation index 2021. Tracking innovation through the COVID-19 crisis*. 14th edition. World Intellectual Property Organization. Available at: https://www.wipo.int/edocs/pubdocs/en/wipo_pub_gii_2021.pdf.

Ekanem, I., & Alrossais, L. A. (2017). Succession challenges facing family businesses in Saudi Arabia. In *Entrepreneurship and business innovation in the Middle East* (pp. 122–146). IGI Global.

Elamin, A. M., & Alomaim, N. (2011). Does organizational justice influence job satisfaction and self-perceived performance in Saudi Arabia work environment. *International Management Review, 7*, 38–49.

Family Capital. (2020a). *The middle east 150: Why family businesses matter so much for the region*. Available at: https://www.famcap.com/the-middle-east-150-why-family-businesses-matter-so-much-for-the-region/.

Family Capital. (2020b). *The world's top 750 family businesses ranking*. Available at: https://www.famcap.com/the-worlds-750-biggest-family-businesses/

Forbes. (2021, May). *Top 100 Arab family businesses in the middle east*. Forbes online. Available at: https://www.forbesmiddleeast.com/lists/top-100-arab-family-businesses-in-the-middle-east-2021/.

GEM. (2022). *Global entrepreneurship monitor 2021/2022 global report opportunity amid disruption*. Available at: https://www.gemconsortium.org/file/open?fileId=50900.

GEM. (2021). *2020/2021 global report*. Available at: https://gemconsortium.org/file/open?fileId=50691

Hofstede, G. H. (2001). *Culture's consequences: Comparing values, behaviors, institutions and organizations across nations*. Sage.

IMD Institute for Management Development. (2021). *IMD world digital competitiveness index 2021, IMD World Competitiveness Center*. Available at: https://www.imd.org/globalassets/wcc/docs/release-2021/digital_2021.pdf

Kalliny, M., & Gentry, L. (2007). Cultural values reflected in Arab and American television advertising. *Journal of Current Issues and Research in Advertising, 29*, 15–32.

Kavoossi, M. (2000). *The globalisation of business and the Middle East: Opportunities and constraints*. Greenwood Publishing Group.

KPMG. (2022). *The power of women in family business. Interviews with women leaders in family businesses in Saudi Arabia*. Available here: https://assets.kpmg/content/dam/kpmg/sa/pdf/2022/the-power-of-women-in-family-business.pdf

KPMG. (2021). *KPMG CEO outlook Saudi Arabia, Purpose-led and prepare the growth*. Available at: https://assets.kpmg/content/dam/kpmg/sa/pdf/2021/ceo-outlook-final-2021.pdf

Krueger, N., Bogers, M. L., Labaki, R., & Basco, R. (2021). Advancing family business science through context theorizing: The case of the Arab world. *Journal of Family Business Strategy, 12*(1), 100377.

Longenecker, J. G., Moore, C. W., Palich, L. E., & Petty, J. W. (2006). *Small business management: An entrepreneurial emphasis*. South-Western Pub.

MAGNITT. (2020). *2020 Saudi Arabia venture capital report*. Available at: https://magnitt.com/research/2020-saudi-arabia-venture-capital-snapshot-50738?utm_source=cta&utm_medium=website&utm_campaign=News

Mellahi, K. (2007). The effect of regulations on HRM: Private sector firms in Saudi Arabia. *The International Journal of Human Resource Management, 18*, 85–99.

Ministry of Commerce and Industry. (2013). *Family business governance manual and indicative charter* (in Arabic), 1s^t draft. Available at: https://chamber.sa/SectoralCommittees/ChamberCommittees/FamilyBusiness/PublishingImages/Pages/Imp_docs/doc_1_familyCompany.pdf

Monshaa't. (2022). *SME monitor, monshaa't quarterly report Q1 2022, monshaa't, small & medium enterprises general authority*. Available at: https://monshaat.gov.sa/sites/default/files/2022-06/Monshaat%20Quarterly%20Report%20Q1%202022%20-%20EN%20%281%29.pdf

Monshaa't. (2020, May 2). The impact of COVID-19 on SME in Saudi Arabia: A large-scale survey. *Monshaa't, White Paper.* 1–32. Available at: https://www.psu.edu.sa/psu/articles/2020/06/25/survey-impact-of-covid-19-on-sme-in-saudi-arabia-white-paper-02_1593062630.pdf

Nurunnabi, M. (2017). Transformation from an oil-based economy to a knowledge-based economy in Saudi Arabia: The direction of Saudi vision 2030. *Journal of the Knowledge Economy, 8*(2), 536–564.

Obeidat, B. Y., Shannak, R. O., Masa'deh, R., & Al-Jarrah, I. (2012). Toward better understanding for Arabian culture: Implications based on Hofstede's cultural model. *European Journal of Social Sciences, 28,* 512–522.

OC&C Strategy Consultants. (2018). *Tech entrepreneurship ecosystem in Kingdom of Saudi Arabia.* Accessed December 10, 2018, from https://s3-eu-west-1.amazonaws.com/wamda-prod/resource-url/2018_KSA_Report_Digital_Version_OC%26C_Updated.pdf

Orient Planet Group. (2020, September). *Resilient leadership: navigating COVID-19 impact on GCC businesses.* Available at: https://www.opresearch.me/FreeReports.html

Palliam, R., Cader, H. A., & Chiemeke, C. (2011). Succession issues among family entrepreneurs in countries of the gulf. *International Journal of Business Administration, 2,* 25.

Pistrui, D., & Fahed-Sreih, J. (2017). Towards an understanding of Islam and Muslim entrepreneurship in the Middle East. In *Entrepreneurship values and responsibility* (pp. 221–234). Routledge.

Poutziouris, P., Smyrnios, K., & Klein, S. (2006). *Handbook of research on family business.* Edward Elgar Pub.

PwC Middle East. (2021). *Middle east family business survey 2021: Diversifying, investing and digitising.* Available at: https://www.pwc.com/m1/en/publications/family-business-survey/2021/documents/middle-east-family-business-survey-2021.pdf

Ramady, M. A. (2010). *The Saudi Arabian economy: Policies, achievements, and challenges, Journal name?* Springer Verlag.

Ramady, M. A., & Sohail, M. S. (2010). Assessing the role of family business in promoting economic growth: Perspectives from Saudi Arabia. *International Journal of Entrepreneurship and Small Business, 10,* 447–459.

Saiz-Alvarez, J. M., Coduras, A., & Roomi, M. A. (2022). Senior entrepreneurship and family business vitality in Saudi Arabia. In *Research anthology on strategies for maintaining successful family firms* (pp. 917–936). IGI Global.

Saudi Council of Economic and Development Affairs (SCEDA). (2016, April 24). *Saudi Vision 2030.* Accessed June 2, 2016, from http://vision2030.gov.sa/download/file/fid/417

Saudi Gazette. (2022). *Saudi Arabia's new companies' law highly flexible, embraces international best practices.* Available at: https://saudigazette.com.sa/article/622367/SAUDI-ARABIA/Saudi-Arabias-new-companies-law-highly-flexible-embraces-international-best-practices

Saudi Gazette. (2018, November 06). Al-Qasibi inaugurates Center for Family enterprises. *Saudi Gazette Report.* Available at: https://saudigazette.com.sa/article/547362

Sfakianakis, J. (2009). Challenges facing family businesses in Saudi Arabia. *ArabNews.* Accessible at: https://www.arabnews.com/node/325450

Strategy&. (2014). *Leveraging an untapped talent pool: How to advance women's role in GCC family businesses.* Alsayedah Khadijah Bint Khuwailid Center. Available at: https://www.ioe-emp.org/fileadmin/ioe_documents/publications/Policy%20Areas/gender/EN/_2016-09-26__Strategy_AKBK_Leveraging_an_untapped_talent_pool.pdf

Shahin, A. I., & Wright, P. L. (2004). Leadership in the context of culture: An Egyptian perspective. *Leadership and Organization Development Journal, 25,* 499–511.

Sharma, P. (2004). An overview of the field of family business studies: Current status and directions for the future. *Family Business Review, 17,* 1–36.

UNDP United Nations Development Programme. (2020). *Human development report 2020. The next frontier. Human Development and the Anthropocene.* http://hdr.undp.org/en/2020-report/download

World Bank. (2020). *Doing business 2020. Comparing business regulation in 190 economies.* Economy profile Saudi Arabia. *Country Report.* Accessed January 12, 2021 from https://www.doingbusiness.org/content/dam/doingBusiness/country/s/saudi-arabia/SAU.pdf

World Economic Forum WEF. (2020). *The Global Competitiveness Report.* Special edition. How countries are performing on the road to recovery. Schwab K., Zahidi, S., Accessed December 25, 2020 from http://www3.weforum.org/docs/WEF_TheGlobalCompetitivenessReport2020.pdf

World Factbook. (2022). *Saudi Country profile.* Available at: https://www.cia.gov/the-world-factbook/countries/saudi-arabia/

Yu, A., Lumpkin, G., Sorenson, R. L., & Brigham, K. H. (2012). The landscape of family business outcomes a summary and numerical taxonomy of dependent variables. *Family Business Review, 25,* 33–57.

Wassim J. Aloulou is an Associate Professor at the College of Economics and Administrative Sciences, Imam Mohammad Ibn Saudi Islamic University, Riyadh, KSA. He received his PhD in Management Sciences from the University of Pierre Mendes, France Grenoble 2, France, and from the Faculté des Sciences Economiques et de Gestion de Sfax, Tunisia in 2008. He teaches graduate and undergraduate courses on entrepreneurship in MBA and BBA programs. His research interests currently focus on digital entrepreneurship, FinTech, entrepreneurial intentions, and orientations of individuals and organizations. He has authored and co-authored multiple articles in reputable international journals (e.g., *European Journal of Innovation Management, Journal of Small Business and Enterprise Development, International Journal of Logistics Management, Journal of Entrepreneurship in Emerging Countries* among others), books with IGI Global on *Business Transformations in the Digital Era* and on *Entrepreneurship and Organizational Resilience* during Unprecedented Times, and multiple book chapters on Incubation, social entrepreneurship, women's economic empowerment, and Entrepreneurial and Business contexts (with Edward Elgar, IGI Global and World Scientific publishers).

Riyadh Alshaeel is an Assistant Professor at the College of Economics and Administrative Sciences, Imam Mohammad Ibn Saudi Islamic University, Riyadh, KSA. He received his PhD in Strategic Management Sciences from Dundee Business School, Scotland, and received his master's degree (MBA) from Edinburgh Business School, Scotland. He teaches graduate and undergraduate courses in research methodology and strategic management in MBA and BBA programs. His research interests currently focus on family business succession and sustainability, the impact of culture and social relations on the family business, and leadership for entrepreneurs' strategy and risk management. He has translated the book *Effective Entrepreneurial Management: Strategy, Planning, Risk Management, and Organization,* into the Arabic language.

Family Business in the United Arab Emirates

Luan Eshtrefi

Abstract Some of the most famous corporations in the world have roots in family business. Ford Motor Company, JP Morgan, and Walmart are just a few examples of family businesses that became large corporations in the United States. Family businesses are the backbone of many economies, including the United Arab Emirates (UAE). These businesses create jobs, add economic value to countries, and are pioneers in entrepreneurship and innovation. This chapter examines why the UAE is the premier country that supports family businesses. By closer view of the business ecosystem in the UAE, the chapter provides insight into five main stakeholders that together create the most effective environment for businesses to prosper. Later, the chapter focuses attention on characteristics of Emirati family businesses and offers some insight into succession in family businesses from one generation to another. The chapter ends with some concluding remarks on how family businesses survived during the pandemic.

1 Introduction

The United Arab Emirates (UAE), a relatively young country that just celebrated its fiftieth birthday, continues to be a leader in the Gulf Cooperation Council (GCC), the Middle East, and even West Asia when it comes to entrepreneurship (Eshtrefi, 2021). Historically, the level of Foreign Direct Investment (FDI) into the UAE has been far higher than any other nation in the region, whether nearby or in the broader region (Dana et. al., 2022). Continuous innovation, flexibility, and attraction make the UAE a certain environment for business to thrive and prosper.

Family-owned businesses provide an important contribution to gross domestic product (GDP) while also employing a significant portion of the global workforce. This can be seen in the UAE. The bulk of the Emirati economy can be contributed to

L. Eshtrefi (✉)
Keller Graduate School of Management, DeVry University, Chicago, USA
e-mail: luan.eshtrefi@devry.edu

© The Author(s), under exclusive license to Springer Nature Switzerland AG 2023
V. Ramadani et al. (eds.), *Family Business in Gulf Cooperation Council Countries*,
Contributions to Management Science,
https://doi.org/10.1007/978-3-031-17262-5_7

family-owned businesses. Family businesses in the UAE are involved in many sectors including automotive, real estate, fashion, and retailing, making them the fabric of the UAE economy (Khansaheb, 2008). Reports indicate that family-owned businesses represent approximately 60% of UAE GDP while employing the vast majority of the country's workforce (Vargese, 2021). This is a significant difference in the makeup of the Emirati economy with the binary Oil–Non-Oil sectors. Fifty years ago, the oil sector made up 90% of the UAE economy while today this sector only makes up 30% of the economy (Ministry of Economy, 2021a). This transformation has yet to occur in many other Gulf countries or other countries in the region.

The Emirati economy has therefore shifted its economy from one based on pure petrochemicals to a diversified economy based on entrepreneurship and innovation, or a knowledge-based economy. The vision of Emirati leaders to develop the nation as a foreign direct investment haven has not only been met but exceeded expectations, by far. An important approach that the UAE has implemented to attract businesses is infrastructure transformation. One particular infrastructure project that can be identified is the Dubai canal. This project spurred business growth and allowed for new developments. Exhibit 1 provides an illustration of the Dubai canal project, which has paved the way for business investments in the surrounding areas.

Many of the foreign businesses that have made the UAE home have chosen this country over others in the region given its forward-looking strategy—supporting business development. Many examples of infrastructure projects can be showcased to influence business development.

This chapter sheds some light on a few topics of family businesses in the UAE. First, a closer examination is offered to illustrate the main stakeholders of the superb business ecosystem in the country. Five main players in the UAE business ecosystem have created an environment in which family businesses in the UAE have thrived. Second, the chapter takes a closer look into the specifics of family businesses in the UAE—highlighting the top family businesses, a closer examination of the Dubai Law on Family Business, and finally noting some perceptions on generational succession in Emirati family businesses. Last, the chapter provides some concluding thoughts on the subject.

2 Business Ecosystem

The UAE is seen as the benchmark country in the GCC, the Middle East, and the broader region when it comes to business support and practices. It has been and continues to be a pioneer in creating a visionary and forward-thinking approach to attract talent, business, and innovation. This has been possible given the business ecosystem that has developed in the UAE in the past three decades.

The UAE has played an instrumental role in engaging the necessary stakeholders as participants in the business ecosystem development for family businesses. The major business ecosystem stakeholders include the UAE Government, UAE free zones, academic institutions, various agencies, and business investors.

Exhibit 1 Dubai Canal, Dubai, United Arab Emirates Source: ©Luan Eshtrefi

These five business ecosystem stakeholders, together, create the right environment for the UAE to continue to lead the region in business growth potential. The UAE government is fast and efficient in enacting legislation to support businesses. UAE free zones have become model organizations for nurturing Emirati businesses. Universities and research institutions in the UAE are offering, more and more, undergraduate teaching and training in entrepreneurship, albeit lagging in family business courses in particular. The small and medium size business support offered through various governmental and nongovernmental agencies has spurred business growth in country. Lastly, the UAE is a haven for venture capital companies that invest heavily in growing companies.

Gulf country governments are unique from other governments around the world given that in many, the decision-making process—enacting legislation—is streamlined, in many cases. The UAE executive government is no different. The Supreme Council of the UAE is the highest decision-making authority in the UAE. This council is made up of the rulers of each of the seven Emirates that constitute the UAE.

Table 1 Members of the Supreme Council of the UAE

• H. H. Sheikh Khalifa bin Zayed Al Nahyan, President of the UAE and Ruler of Abu Dhabi
• H. H. Sheikh Mohammed bin Rashid Al Maktoum, Vice President and Prime Minister of the UAE and Ruler of Dubai
• H. H. Sheikh Sultan bin Mohammed Al Qasimi, Ruler of Sharjah
• H. H. Sheikh Humaid bin Rashid Al Nuami, Ruler of Ajman
• H. H. Sheikh Saud bin Rashid Al Mualla, Ruler of Umm Al Quwain
• H. H. Sheikh Saud bin Saqr Al Qasimi, Ruler of Ras Al Khaimah
• H. H. Sheikh Hamad bin Mohammed Al Sharqi, Ruler of Fujairah.

Source: Government of Dubai (2021)

The UAE has a unique political system given that it does not possess political parties. The UAE is rather ruled by the Supreme Council, the highest constitutional authority of the UAE. Table 1 illustrates the eight current members of the Supreme Council.

The UAE President and Head of State, H.H. Sheikh Khalifa, has not made a public appearance in many years. The Crown Prince of Abu Dhabi, H.H. Mohammed bin Zayed Al Nahyan, has taken on his brother's role in the Supreme Council until any further notice to the public will be made on succession to the Ruler of Abu Dhabi. As the Crown Prince of Abu Dhabi, it is assumed that H.H. Mohammed bin Zayed Al Nahyan will be chosen as the next President of the UAE. Exhibit 2 shows the Presidential Palace from afar, a symbol of the house of the Zayed and the rulership of Abu Dhabi.

The Prime Minister of the UAE, who is coincidently the Vice President and Minister of Defence, is also simultaneously the ruler of Dubai, H.H. Sheikh Mohammed bin Rashid Al Maktoum (Government of Dubai, 2021).

As a federation, much emphasis is placed on local government initiatives in the country. Each of the seven emirates has its own local government and local government legislation and initiatives. The UAE's constitution defines the working relationship between federal and local governments and allows some flexibility in the distribution of authority and scope of work between them in line with the vision of the leadership at the highest levels (Government of Dubai, 2021).

The UAE Ministry of Economy has developed strategies to continue to welcome small and medium size (SME) companies. Table 2 showcases the UAE Ministry of Economy's eight work directives to support SMEs.

One of the most important elements as shown in Table 2 is the fact that the Ministry of Economy has clear intentions to help Emirati businesses succeed in the market. This can be seen in all directives, but a particular emphasis is placed on Emirati-owned businesses as first priority in bidding for and winning UAE government contracts.

Moreover, the Ministry of Economy has also published the various themes of the UAE national agenda for entrepreneurship and SMEs. The seven themes are very much related to one another in that there is clear cohesion and a general theme: How

Exhibit 2 Presidential Palace, Abu Dhabi, United Arab Emirates ©Luan Eshtrefi

Table 2 Eight work directives to support SMEs

1	Constant review of business environment based on requirements of start-ups.
2	Facilitating the process of establishing small and medium-sized enterprises in the UAE.
3	Providing knowledge and inspiration for future generations to start their own businesses.
4	Supporting the productivity of SMEs and improving their performance.
5	Giving priority to Emirati-owned companies in government contracts.
6	Increasing the contribution of SMEs to the GDP.
7	Attracting international technology start-ups.
8	Accelerating the transformation of start-ups into public joint stock companies.

Source: Ministry of Economy (2021a)

can the UAE government support local entrepreneurs and help them create innovative businesses that can thrive? Table 3 lists the seven themes.

All seven themes are necessary to increase business growth, but themes one and six are highlighted here. The UAE has been a real pioneer in creating legislation to support businesses. A recent example of the Emirati experience in how legislation keeps up with innovation is the UAE initiative Regulations Lab or RegLab. RegLab works with regulators and the private sector, including innovators and business leaders, to co-create legislation that is in step with the speed of innovation (Regulations Lab, 2022). Later in the chapter, we will see how the Dubai Emirate spearheaded the Law on Family Business, for example. Theme six is also addressed

Table 3 Seven themes of the UAE National Agenda for entrepreneurship and SMEs

Theme	Action
1. Ease of doing business	Reviewing and developing legislation and policies to facilitate doing business
2. Innovation	Stimulating innovation in priority economic sectors
3. Business support.	Providing solutions to support SMEs and increasing their efficiency
4. Digital transformation	Building a supportive environment and developing incentives that support digital transformation
5. Funding	Providing various channels for financing start-ups and SMEs
6. Human capital	Encouraging various segments of society to enter the field of entrepreneurship
7. Increasing demand	Enable SMEs to access different markets

Source: Ministry of Economy (2021a)

below by research and universities in the country providing students of all majors learning experiences in concrete business principles irrespective of university major.

One of the most contemporary examples of how the UAE Government is a major stakeholder in the business ecosystem is its efficient management of the pandemic. The global public health crisis in 2020 brought on by the novel Coronavirus (COVID-19) created some of the most difficult challenges for households and businesses around the world, including the UAE. The incentives and measures taken by the UAE government include a diverse set of policy initiatives and tools to support large companies, SMEs, entrepreneurs, and other economic enterprises (Ministry of Economy, 2020). Table 4 provides a snapshot of some of the expansionary monetary and fiscal policies provided by the UAE Central Bank and federal government respectively to support businesses and households during the worst months of the pandemic.

The four expansionary monetary and three expansionary fiscal policies addressed in Table 4 above clearly illustrate the seriousness and effective economic stimulus and market liquidity provided by the federal government and central bank of the UAE. The unprecedented liquidity by the UAE Central Bank was well accepted by many businesses while the fiscal stimulus by the UAE federal government supported household consumption and thus aggregate demand. A reduction of base interest rates, bank reserve requirements, and liquidity to commercial banks simultaneously calmed markets and provided market liquidity as well.

Given the nature of the UAE as a federal organization, the seven Emirates have also provided specific local fiscal expansionary relief, specifically to businesses operating in the respective Emirate. A closer examination of the financial support of the Government of Dubai is provided in Table 5. The Government of Dubai launched a package of economic incentives worth AED 1.5 billion that includes 15 initiatives serving specific sectors to support businesses during the worst months of the pandemic.

Table 4 Highlights of Expansionary Monetary and Fiscal Policies of the UAE Federal Government

Expansionary Monetary Policy Initiative → UAE Central Bank reduced the monetary policy interest rate twice since the beginning of 2020, with a total value of 125 basis points.
Expansionary Monetary Policy Initiative → Line of credit to commercial banks in the UAE amounting to AED 50 billion at zero cost.
Expansionary Monetary Policy Initiative → Reduction of Reserve Ratio of demand deposits by half, from 14% to 7%, which will enhance liquidity and inject an estimated AED 61 billion of liquidity in the banking sector for new loans.
Expansionary Monetary Policy Initiative → Other liquidity mechanisms for private sector borrowers such as temporary exemption from principal and interest payments on existing loans, new regulations to reduce fees on debit or credit cards, and new regulations setting limits for fees imposed by banks on SMEs including the removal of the minimum balance threshold.
Expansionary Fiscal Policy Initiative → Fiscal stimulus valued at AED 16 billion to support business continuity and provide additional stimulus for the national economy.
Expansionary Fiscal Policy Initiative → Fiscal stimulus package aimed at businesses includes reduction of electricity and water consumption bills by 20% for select sectors, freezing utility fines, postponing instalment fees, and extending deadlines for financial disclosures.
Expansionary Fiscal Policy Initiative → Fiscal stimulus package aimed at households includes extending residency permits, halt on administrative fines, extending government services, and allowing vehicle registration without paying fines.

Source: Ministry of Economy (2020)

Table 5 Highlights of the Dubai Government Fiscal Expansionary Policies

→ Refunding a portion of the 5% customs tariff paid for imported goods that are sold locally.
→ Reducing costs related to registration, licensing, and related administrative fees by half or more for companies operating at Jebel Ali Free Zone.
→ Exempting companies from fees of new sales permits and commercial offers in order to boost foreign trade and enhance competitiveness.
→ Renewing commercial licenses without obligatory renewal of lease contracts and cancelling applicant fee down payments.
→ Reducing municipality fee by half on hotel sales, a reduction from 7% to 3.5%.
→ Postponing rent payment up to six months.

Source: Ministry of Economy (2020)

The fiscal stimulus package offered by the Dubai Government in the early months of the pandemic eased pressures on businesses that were experiencing the economic shocks not seen in recent history. One of the most important stimulus issues was that offered to the entertainment industry, reducing municipality fees in half. Given the importance of tourism in Dubai, the hotel industry greatly benefited from these macroeconomic policy tools. In particular, the Jumeriah Beach Residence development in Dubai, as depicted in Exhibit 3, is one of many example areas in Dubai that required fiscal relief in order to ensure continued business activity.

Without going into much detail, various economic Free Zones have also implemented fiscal stimulus packages for businesses that operate in those various areas across the nation. The UAE free zone authorities provided further relief to

Exhibit 3 Jumeriah Beach Residence Area, Dubai, United Arab Emirates ©Luan Eshtrefi

businesses and tenants. The below will highlight the importance of UAE free zones as yet another important stakeholder in the business ecosystem.

The UAE is a leader in attracting foreign direct investment given its commitment and development of economic free zones. The UAE has over 40 free zones, allowing full foreign ownership of a business in the UAE (Invest in UAE, 2020). This ownership structure has revolutionized the old local content requirement of the need to obtain local partnership with Emirati companies or citizens that needed to provide sponsorship of foreign companies wishing to do business in the UAE. This

Table 6 A snapshot of some free zones in Dubai based on category

Name	Category
Dubai Maritime City	Maritime Services
Dubai Commercity	E-Commerce
Dubai Textile City	Textiles
Dubai South	Artificial Intelligence and Futuristic Activities
Dubai Airport Free Zone	Mixed-use
Dubai World Trade Centre	Events and Conferences
Dubai Design District	Creative Design
Dubai Science Park	Scientific Research
International Humanitarian City	Humanitarian Hub
Dubai Multi Commodities Centre	Commodity Trade
Dubai Outsource City	eCommerce and Support Services
Dubai Silicon Oasis	Technology
Dubai International Financial Centre	Financial Hub
Dubai Internet City	Technology
Meydan Free Zone	Mixed use
Dubai Healthcare City	Healthcare
Dubai International Academic City	Academic
Dubai Production City	Media
Dubai Studio City	Media
Dubai Media City	Media

Source: Ministry of Economy (2021b)

has relaxed regulations on businesses entering the UAE from abroad, but also paved a new path for local businesses as well.

Over 50% of all UAE free zones are found in two particular Emirates: Dubai and Abu Dhabi. Independent free zone authorities (FZAs) govern these unique districts and are solely responsible for issuing operating licenses and supporting business establishment (English Business Council, 2020). In other words, free zones can be considered as micro governments within the local government structure of any particular Emirate. Procedures for establishing free zone international businesses are quick and efficient given the support they receive from the respective FZA authority they operate in.

Table 6 illustrates 20 free zones that operate in the Emirate of Dubai. A closer examination of any of these state-of-the-art free zones showcases the interest made by SMEs to obtain space. For example, the Dubai Airport Free zone or DAFZA is a mixed-use type of free zone strategically located next to the Dubai International Airport. As shown in Exhibit 4, DAFZA boasts over 1800 businesses operating in dozens of sectors and various industries with nearly 20,000 workers, who benefit from a business-focused regulatory and tax environment that offers full ownership and complete repatriation of earnings to the businesses' home country (DAFZA, 2021). Many free zones in the region have copied the footprint of DAFZA, creating free zones in or around international airports and terminals has had tremendous

Exhibit 4 Dubai Airport Free Zone, Dubai, United Arab Emirates ©Luan Eshtrefi

effects on products being loaded off airplanes and into retail shops with great efficiency and ease.

The third in a series of stakeholders or parties involved in creating the vibrant ecosystem in the UAE are universities and research institutions. One of the most innovative policy shifts in the UAE includes the obligation for higher education institutions to provide more learning opportunities in entrepreneurship and family business. This moves forth the Emiratization process, or the desire for the UAE Government to support more Emirati nationals to enter the private sector employment. Most Gulf countries have initiated a similar policy to transform local citizenry into private sector employment, however, the UAE has seen real and measured change.

In order to foster Emiratization, all public universities at the national level are obliged to offer specific courses to Emirati nationals—no matter their undergraduate major. This aims with UAE policy to incorporate an entrepreneurial oriented perspective in higher education (Basco, 2021). However, research suggests that too few courses are offered in the family business in Emirati universities for far too small a group of students, noting the need to create a roadmap by the Ministry of Education for higher education institutions in the country (Basco, 2021). Basco et al. (2021) also triangulates the relationship between student, university, and UAE government by addressing University management in altering educational programs to include family business education into curriculums, perhaps as entrepreneurship and innovation courses have been implemented in various departments and majors, not necessarily related to business-oriented programs.

In particular, the United Arab Emirates University (UAEU) can be seen as a benchmark educational institution that supports an innovation ecosystem by developing research in health and space sciences while also attracting business start-ups and setting up business incubators (Debbage & Al Kaabi, 2019). The take here is that Emirati universities are addressing the real need to offer all undergraduates some business training, whether these students study business, engineering, health sciences, or other disciplines. This is something that many other Gulf countries have yet to plan or implement.

Yet another important stakeholder in the UAE business ecosystem includes support agencies (governmental and non-governmental) that have supported local businesses with vast amounts of capital and expertise. Emirati businesses can receive special support for growth from various government and nongovernment agencies. These businesses, owned by Emirati nationals, have specialized treatment from at least eight agencies, backed by government funding, either local government funding or federal funding. Table 7 illustrates the agency fund name and some basic information for each fund.

Although all eight agencies support local businesses in the UAE, one, in particular, stands out. The Khalifa Fund for Enterprise Development has provided a staggering AED 1.32 billion in funds for local businesses and provides tailor-made trainings on business financing. This organization is considered the model agency that UAE businesses turn to for support. Another large agency that supports Emirati businesses is the Mohammed Bin Rashid Innovation Fund (MBRIF). MBRIF is a federal agency initiative sponsored by the federal government of the UAE, via the Ministry of Finance, to support innovators with affordable government-backed financing (Ministry of Finance, 2021). The significant financing that MBRIF provides to local businesses topped a total of AED 2 billion up to date. Last, the Emirates Development Bank (EBD) backs start-ups and micro-businesses with loans and business support, with an impressive AED 1.8 billion in loans to 550 companies in the UAE (Ministry of Economy, 2021c). And the ambitions of the EBD are to provide AED 30 billion in business loans to 13,500 businesses, with an extra AED 10 billion in extra contribution to UAE GDP (Emirates Development Bank, 2021). The stunning increase in business loans by the EBD in the next few years signifies the increasing interest of this agency to support Emirati businesses.

Other than government, university, free zone authority, and nonprofit stakeholders, venture capital companies have an important role in the business ecosystem. The UAE boasts hundreds of private equity companies that heavily invest in business start-ups and those with scaling potential. Table 8 provides a list of the top seven venture capital business investors in the UAE based on the number and volume of capital provided.

Altogether, these various venture capital companies have provided over USD 235 million in funding to local businesses in the UAE. Most venture capital companies in the region have their headquarters in the UAE given the excellent infrastructure and environment. As depicted in Table 8, Wamda Capital provided significant capital to LambdaTest, Nana, and Tamatem companies, totalling USD 37.5 million in funding in Both Series A and B financing rounds.

Table 7 Eight agencies that support Emirati-owned businesses

Agency	Business support brief	Activities
Khalifa Fund for Enterprise Development	Aims at encouraging entrepreneurship, inculcating the culture of innovation, and supporting the SMEs, KFED is running several highly targeted financing and training initiatives	AED 1.32 billion in loans and over 900 workshops to promote business development
Mohammed Bin Rashid Establishment for SME Development (Dubai SME)	Offers a wide range of services to entrepreneurs and businesspersons right from planning a project to reaching its full potential	AED 823 million in financial incentives to date
Sharjah Foundation to Support Pioneering Entrepreneurs (RUWAD)	Provides financial and technical support to entrepreneurs and small businesses in the emirate, creating a business-focussed environment for effective development of projects	Over 400 projects in 2019 and 2020 combined and more than 5300 professionals and business owners trained
Taziz Programme for the development of SMEs by Ajman Department of Economic Development	Aims to encourage citizens to engage in economic activity, support their projects, create more job opportunities, provide an investment environment that incubates entrepreneurship and develops small and medium enterprises	More than 450 registered members and over 800 individuals trained
Saud Bin Saqr Establishment for Youth Enterprise Development	Aims to nurture youth entrepreneurship and develop an SME culture, thereby focusing on diversification of UAE's national economy	Over 3000 beneficiaries and over 800 training courses to date
Sharjah Entrepreneurship Centre (Sheraa)	Established to support the business environment incubating entrepreneurship in Sharjah and aims to stimulate the establishment and growth of start-up companies	Over USD 130 million revenue generated by Sheraa supported companies and over USD 87 million capital raised
Mohammed Bin Rashid Innovation Fund	Aims to achieve the goals of the National Innovation Strategy, fill the funding gap in innovation projects, and attract the best talents of start-up companies from all over the world	AED 2 billion in capital provides support in certain sectors of the National Innovation Strategy
Emirates Development Bank	Established to meet the goals of the national agenda to create and offer financing solutions with flexible terms for SMEs	AED 1.8 billion in business loans provided to 550 companies

Source: Ministry of Economy (2021c)

Table 8 Top venture capital companies operating in the UAE by number of investments

Investor name	Brief information	Latest investment rounds
Wamda Capital	A leading regional Venture Capital Firm focused on deploying growth capital in the Middle East and North Africa's leading entrepreneur-led technology companies	LambdaTest: Venture capital (Series B) ($16 M) Nana: Venture capital (Series B) ($18 M) Tamatem: Venture capital (Series A) ($3.5 M)
500 Global	A venture capital firm that invests early in founders building fast-growing technology companies	FarMart: Venture capital (Series A) ($10 M) Productfy: Venture capital (Series A) ($16 M) Sarwa: Venture capital (Series B) ($15 M)
Middle East Venture Partners	A venture capital firm that invests in the early stages of innovative technology companies run by talented entrepreneurs in Beirut, Dubai, and throughout the MENA region	VertoFX: Venture capital (Series A) ($10 M) Sarwa: Venture capital (Series B) ($15 M) Bykea: Venture capital (Series B) ($13 M)
BECO Capital	A leading MENA venture capital investor, focused primarily on the GCC and based in Dubai, investing in technology companies from the seed stage onwards	Taager: Seed fund ($6.4 M) MaxAB: Venture capital (Series A) ($40 M) Proximie: Venture capital (Series B) ($38 M)
STC Ventures	A venture capital fund investing in IT, telecommunications, and digital media, investing across the MENA region and internationally	YallaCompare: Venture capital (Series C) ($8M) yallacompare: Venture capital (Series C) ($8M) yallacompare: Venture capital (Series B) ($3.5 M)
Jabbar Internet Group	A venture capital in the consumer e-commerce sector in the Arab World	Kitchenful: Venture capital (Series A) ($1.9 M) Arzooo.com: Venture capital (Series A) ($7.5 M) GrocerApp: Seed fund ($1 M)
Shorooq Investments	A leading technology investor in the Middle East, North Africa, and Pakistan	Clara: Seed fund ($2 M) RentSher: Venture capital ($1.1 M) joi Gifts: Seed fund ($1.5 M)

Source: Index (2021)

Another significant investment can be seen by the venture capital company Global 500, which has also provided significant financing to three Emirati companies in the amount of USD 41 million, namely to FarMart, Productfy, and Sarwa companies, respectively.

3 Family Business

Well before the glamour and lour of Dubai or the UAE, family businesses have been an important part of the UAE economy. Even before it gained independence from the British crown, the UAE had many successful family-owned businesses. This section of the chapter examines family businesses in the UAE and showcases many successful Emirati companies. Moreover, a look into the contemporary issues of Emirati family businesses along with generational succession challenges. These issues are not faced only in the UAE—family businesses all over the world have similar successes and challenges.

Table 9 provides a synopsis of the top 10 family businesses in the UAE for 2020, ranked by Forbes Middle East (Forbes Middle East, 2021). What is striking from this list is the fact that all of the top 10 listed companies are Emirati family businesses owned, that is, these are local companies established and owned by Emirati nationals and have, or will have, generational family succession.

Second, all companies are diversified in the sectors and industries they serve and operate in. In terms of wealth, these are the most capital-wealthy companies in the UAE, and many are even benchmarked as capital wealthy in the GCC. In the region, the top 10 family-owned businesses employ over half a million workers and comprise a total net worth of over USD 31 billion (Vargese, 2021).

The most successful Emirati family business, now a conglomerate company, is also one of the oldest companies in the country. The Al-Futtaim Group was founded over 90 years ago and has achieved much success—it has brought the family ownership to over USD 2 billion in wealth. This sparked another division for the family with Majid Al Futtaim company, now listed on Forbes Middle East as the second-ranked family business in the UAE (Forbes Middle East, 2021). The Al-Futtaim family, therefore, controls both first and second place in the Forbes Middle East Rankings for the UAE.

The same circumstances seem feasible for the Al-Ghurair conglomerate. Another company that was founded decades ago involved in real estate, food industry, and then moved to the finance industry coming in at a third place in the top 10 Forbes list (Forbes Middle East, 2021). These family-owned businesses are worth billions and are considered not only top companies in the UAE but also in the Arab world.

To top off the top five Emirate family businesses, the Lootah group has impressive construction projects that support the development of many areas in the UAE. Most notably, Lootah Group is constructing a 700-megawatt solar hybrid project in Mohammad Bin Rashid Al Maktoum Solar Park, Dubai, one of the largest solar park construction projects in the Gulf (Lootah Group, 2021). Other notable Emirati

Table 9 Forbes Middle East: UAE's Top 10 Family Businesses in 2020

Rank	Company	Establishment and leadership	Quick facts
1.	Al-Futtaim Group	1930—Abdullah Al Futtaim, net worth of >USD 2.1 billion	Al-Futtaim Group today has >200 businesses in sectors including automotive, financial services, real estate, retail, and health categories
2.	Majid Al Futtaim	1992—Majid Al Futtaim, net worth of >USD 3.3 billion	Retailing and entertainment giant currently owns and operates 27 shopping malls and 13 hotels
3.	Al-Ghurair	1960—Abdul Aziz Abdulla Al Ghurair, net worth of USD 3.7 billion	Portfolio includes Al Ghurair Properties, Al Ghurair Foods, and founded Mashreq Bank
4.	Al-Ghurair Group	1960—Abdul Rahman Saif Al Ghurair	Real estate portfolio, petrochemical business for food packaging. The group is also involved in metal manufacturing through Al Ghurair Iron and Steel
5.	S.S. Lootah Group	1956—Yahya Lootah	Founded Dubai Islamic Bank and established the UAE's first contracting company and medical college. Other businesses include construction, energy, real estate, food and hospitality, and healthcare sectors
6.	Juma Al Majid Holding Group	1950—Juma Al Majid	Consists of 33 companies operating in automotive, shipping, real estate, contracting, construction, FMCG, and travel
7.	AW Rostamani Group	1954—Khalid Al Rostamani	Fourteen companies representing automotive, real estate and construction, retail, logistics, information technology, travel, and consultancy
8.	Easa Al Gurg Group	1960—Easa Saleh Al Gurg	Group's portfolio today has 27 companies and > 370 international brands, including Osram, SieMatic, British American Tobacco, Dunlop, Danfoss, Smeg, and 3 M
9.	Al Habtoor Group	1970—Khalaf Al Habtoor	Sectors such as hospitality, automotive and car-leasing, real estate, education, and publishing
10.	Al Naboodah Holding	1958—Abdullah Mohammed Juma Al Naboodah	Other than construction, the group is into automobile, travel, electrical, logistics, agriculture, fit-out, and renewable energy

Source: Forbes Middle East (2021)

businesses not on the list include those that are not considered family businesses but are well-known national companies, such as Emaar, one of the largest construction companies in the UAE but also in the Middle East which is most notable for constructing the landmark Bur Khalifa in Dubai, the tallest building in the world

Exhibit 5 Burj Khalifa, Dubai, United Arab Emirates ©Luan Eshtrefi

as shown in Exhibit 5. As of May 2021, Emaar has a market capitalization of USD 7.6 billion (Forbes, 2021).

One of the many reasons the UAE continues to have family business success stories is because of the support and efficiency of the government. Understanding that, the top family businesses were on the verge of having succession phases from one generation to another, the authorities drafted and enacted laws to support these family businesses.

Family businesses need to grow in order to maintain healthy business prospects. PwC Middle East suggests that family businesses that have endured and prospered on those that have put in place clear legal structures and governance mechanisms aimed at ensuring growth and continuity (PwC Middle East, 2019). Moreover, if

Table 10 Family considerations to exit a family business

→ Perceived unfairness between active and passive family members
→ Family conflict
→ Issues around family members working in the business
→ Choosing future leaders of the family and business (succession considerations)
→ Liquidation of assets / cash-out decision for departing shareholder
→ Shareholder seeking personal or professional fulfilment outside of the family business

Source: PwC Middle East (2019)

Table 11 Dubai Family Law Nr. 9 of 2020 Objectives

1. Developing a comprehensive and clear legal framework to regulate family ownership in the Emirate and facilitate its smooth and easy transmission among successive generations.
2. Maintaining the continuity of family ownership and enhancing the role it plays in achieving economic and social growth in the Emirate.
3. Maintaining social cohesion and avoiding anything that might provoke disputes among members of the same family.
4. Reuniting family members in strong and solid partnerships that can compete in all economic activities and motivating them to serve society, particularly in the fields of education, health, and culture.
5. Fulfilling the needs of development and growth, by developing the capacity of young leaders from succeeding generations to administer family property and enabling them to benefit from the experience of parents and grandparents.

Source: Trowers and Hamlins (2021)

business growth is not achieved, new generations may not achieve similar wealth as the previous generation. Of the many family considerations for exiting a family-owned business, a few major reasons are highlighted in Table 10.

Family members exit a family business based on some of the reasons shown above in Exhibit 15. Perceptions of who, from the family owners, works harder, can trickle down to family conflicts and the business could easily suffer. Given the vast experience of family business in the UAE, and given the country's lead position in the Gulf, the UAE has been the pioneer in attempting to create more effective and efficient growth strategies for its family businesses.

In August 2020, His Highness Sheikh Mohammed bin Rashid Al Maktoum, Ruler of Dubai, Vice President, and Prime Minister of the UAE, issued Law No. (9) of 2020. This law created a new law that regulates the way family businesses operate (PwC Middle East, 2021). The law sets out to promote the preservation, sustainability, and scalability of a family's wealth in a business while also promoting smooth cohesion among family members, ensuring a smooth transition of the family business from generation to generation (Omari, 2020). The objectives of the Family Business Law are provided in Table 11.

In the GCC, approximately 80% of family businesses are at a critical transition phase of first to second, or second to third generations (Alghanim, 2021). Being aware of this, bright minds in the UAE have decided to support family businesses, for example, by enacting legislation such as that of the Dubai Family Law.

The Law contains specific provisions for risk mitigation in management and ownership as a family business transition from one generation to another (Hammadeh, 2020). The first objective alone of the new law on family business notes the need to provide the new generation of the family business ease in succession.

One of the biggest challenges for family businesses in the Middle East lies in family relationships. There have been hints of an increase in family conflicts of family businesses in the Middle East, although the respect held for the older generation, has helped to contain conflict somehow (PwC Middle East, 2021). Moreover, many family businesses in the Middle East are also reaching a critical succession phase as second-generation family members have already become majority shareholders in more than 50% of businesses in the region (PwC Middle East, 2021). This is exactly why the Dubai Emirate acted correctly to create a more precise family business law in order to preserve the succession of family ownership of businesses from one generation to the next.

Considering next-generation family business owners, studies indicate the lack of interest of the next generation (NextGen) in succession. In a study conducted by the American University of Sharjah, in which 200 respondents whose parents had family businesses in the UAE, only one-fifth of NextGen's had an intention to join their family businesses (Basco et al., 2021). This strikingly low number needs further analysis on the reasons which leads NextGens away from the family business. It is worth noting, however, that the percentage of NextGens that intend to take over the family business drops further in the Arab world and more so in the rest of the world (Basco et al., 2021).

4 Concluding Remarks

This chapter has provided insight into family businesses in the UAE. First, the chapter showcased the five business ecosystem stakeholders that have supported small businesses in the UAE. The UAE Government, free zone authorities, university and research institutions, support agencies, and venture capital companies, have together made the business ecosystem the most dynamic in the Arab world, by far.

Second, the chapter particularly focused on family businesses in the UAE, highlighting the top performing Emirati businesses, the chapter provided information on the similarities and differences between the big ten. The chapter provided insight into some of the main reasons for family business conflict and why some family members exit the business. The chapter also focused on specific measures taken in Dubai to ensure smooth generational succession with new legislation to ensure business continuity. The UAE should take initiative to enact the Dubai Law on Family Business in all seven Emirates in order to standardize family business planning efficiency. The section ended with some information on how NextGens perceive their role in the family business in the UAE as the carriers of the baton as older generations of the family businesses retire.

The main issue now with UAE family businesses is the pandemic risks. In a recent study of nearly 2500 family business owners from around the world, nearly 70% of the respondents reported revenue losses during COVID-19, with those family businesses in the Middle East and Africa reporting a staggering 84% of revenue losses (KPMG, 2021). The pandemic had a particular effect on the UAE economy, given its economic diversity into tourism, among others. This prompted the unprecedented fiscal stimulus to bring economies out of deep recession but also support family businesses. In the same study addressed above, more than three-quarters of family businesses globally accessed some form of government subsidies or other forms of financial support—43% acquired financial support while 36% made use of tax reduction and tax filing deferral opportunities (KPMG, 2021).

As a result, the UAE has handled the pandemic in a more efficient way than other governments in the Gulf or wider Arab world. At the height of the pandemic, the UAE has had consistently low death rates per million inhabitants than, for example, the United Kingdom (Statisa, 2020). With innovative ways to maintain low levels of positive infection of the virus such as contract tracing, digitalization of multiple government agencies, and innovation in the education sector, the UAE was able to reopen its borders to tourists in mid-2020 (KPMG, 2020). Given the significant proportion of the UAE economy related to tourism, this is an encouraging development. It remains to be seen how the different variants of the virus may affect COVID-19 policy or even results, however.

This chapter has showcased the UAE as the place for family businesses to thrive. Given its strategic location in the Middle East, the infrastructure available, and economic diversity, the UAE will continue to stand out in a crowd of nations as a place where family businesses will continue to thrive. Looking toward the future of family business in the UAE and the Middle East, some clear conclusions have been observed as shown in a survey of 2801 family businesses in the region. Notably, the top priorities of more than half of the family businesses are planning to expand into new markets or client segments (PwC, 2021). Lastly, in terms of new urgency during the pandemic, 75% of surveyed respondents noted that digital, technology, and innovation initiatives are key priorities for family businesses (PwC, 2021). This shift to digitization and technology will move family businesses to new heights in both the UAE and the region. Especially for the UAE, where digitization and technology have been part of the business ecosystem for years.

References

Alghanim, O. (2021, May). The family way: How the Gulf could create a more sustainable private sector. *CEO Middle East*. Accessed Dec 12, 2021, from https://www.ceo-middleeast.com/innovation/463156-how-the-gulf-could-could-create-more-sustainable-private-sector

Basco, R. (2021). Why undergraduates in the UAE should learn about their family business. *The National News*. Accessed Nov 28, 2021, from https://www.thenationalnews.com/opinion/comment/2021/10/26/why-undergraduates-in-the-uae-should-learn-about-their-family-business/

Basco, R., Hamdan, R., & Vyas, A. (2021). *Succession intention of the United Arab Emirates next gens*. American University of Sharjah.

DAFZA. (2021). *Dubai Airport Free zone: Launch Your Business*. Accessed Dec 01, 2021, from https://www.dafz.ae/en/business-space/rental-office-space/

Dana, L. P., Salamzadeh, A., & Ramadani, V. (2022). *Understanding contexts of business in Western Asia: Land of bazaars and high-tech booms*. World Scientific.

Debbage, K. & K. Al Kaabi (2019). A UAE recipe for success: Building an effective entrepreneurial ecosystem. *Gulf News*. Accessed Feb 15, 2021, from https://gulfnews.com/opinion/a-uae-recipe-for-success-building-an-effective-entrepreneurial-ecosystem-1.67262519#

Emirates Development Bank. (2021). Accessed Dec 5, 2021, from https://www.edb.gov.ae/en

English Business Council. (2020). *Doing business in the UAE*. Accessed Dec 01, 2021, from https://www.englishbusinesscouncil.com/doing-business-in-the-uae/

Eshtrefi, L. (2021). Entrepreneurship in the United Arab Emirates. In Dana, L-P., R. Palalic, and Ramadani, V. (Eds). Entrepreneurship in the Gulf cooperation council: Evolution and future perspectives. : World Scientific.

Forbes. (2021). *Emaar properties*. Accessed Dec 11, 2021, from https://www.forbes.com/companies/emaar-properties/?sh=26765ccfe1b8

Forbes Middle East. (2021). *The UAE's top 10 family businesses 2020*. Accessed Dec 11, 2021, from https://www.forbesmiddleeast.com/leadership/leaders/uaes-top-ten-family-businesses

Government of Dubai. (2021). *Media office: The United Arab Emirates*. Accessed Dec 15, 2021, from https://www.mediaoffice.ae/general-information/the-united-arab-emirates

Hammadeh, F. (2020, September). *Family ownership law: A legacy of resilience, family business council-gulf*. Accessed Dec 16, 2021, from https://www.fbc-gulf.org/mediafiles/articles/doc-1611-2020_09_24_01_04_41.pdf

Index. (2021). *United Arab Emirates list of venture capital companies*. Accessed Dec 16, 2021, from https://index.co/country/united-arab-emirates/investors

Invest in UAE. (2020) *The UAE: An ideal investment destination and partner*. Accessed Dec 14, 2021, from https://visituae.economy.ae/investment/en/old-en/competitive-edge-of-the-uae.html

Khansaheb, A. (2008). Internationalization of Family Businesses in the UAE. *The British University of Dubai*. Accessed Oct 10, 2021, from https://bspace.buid.ac.ae/bitstream/handle/1234/302/20050020.pdf;jsessionid=63409A0B5932E35C4BA04D3A2F42FD6B?sequence=1

KPMG. (2021). *Mastering a comeback: How family businesses are triumphing over COVID-19*. Accessed Dec 17, 2021, from https://home.kpmg/content/dam/kpmg/xx/pdf/2021/03/family-business-survey-report.pdf

KPMG. (2020). *COVID 19 government measures of the UAE*. Accessed Dec 18, 2021, from https://home.kpmg/ae/en/home/insights/2020/08/covid-19-government-measures-uae.html

Lootah Group. (2021). *700–250 MW Hybrid Project*. Accessed Dec 1, 2021, from https://lootahgroup.com/700-250-mw-hybrid-project/

Ministry of Economy. (2021a). *United Arab Emirates*. The UAE Economy Indicators. Accessed Dec 14, 2021, from https://www.moec.gov.ae/en/economic-indices

Ministry of Economy. (2021b) *United Arab Emirates*. More than 40 multidisciplinary free zones in the UAE. Accessed Dec 14, 2021, from https://www.moec.gov.ae/en/free-zones?emirate=101581

Ministry of Economy. (2021c). *United Arab Emirates. Entities Supporting Projects of Emirati Entrepreneurs*. Accessed Dec 01, 2021, from https://www.moec.gov.ae/en/entrepreneurship-support-entities

Ministry of Economy. (2020). *The annual economic report 2020*, 28th Edition. Accessed Dec 01, 2021, from https://www.moec.gov.ae/documents/20121/302471/English%20Version%20_MOE_Annual%20Report.pdf/e89802b5-b321-126f-ccae-62c2103cac5b

Ministry of Finance. (2021). *United Arab Emirates: Mohammed Bin Rashid Innovation Fund.* Accessed Dec 16, 2021, from https://www.mof.gov.ae/en/About/programsProjects/Pages/MohamedBinRashidInnovationBox.aspx

Omari, Y. (2020). What is Dubai's new family business law and why has it been introduced? *The national news.* Accessed Oct 9, 2021, from https://www.thenationalnews.com/business/comment/what-is-dubai-s-new-family-business-law-and-why-has-it-been-introduced-1.1081028

PwC Middle East. (2021). *Middle East family business survey 2021: diversifying, investing and digitising.* Accessed Dec 14, 2021, from https://www.pwc.com/m1/en/publications/family-business-survey/2021/documents/middle-east-family-business-survey-2021.pdf

PwC Middle East. (2021). *UAE: Introduction of Dubai family ownership law.* Accessed Dec 13, 2021, from https://www.pwc.com/m1/en/services/tax/me-tax-legal-news/2020/uae-introduction-dubai-family-ownership-law.html

PwC Middle East. (2019, April). *Family business shareholder exit strategies and valuation principles.* Accessed Dec 16, 2021, from https://www.fbc-gulf.org/mediafiles/articles/doc-1495-2019_05_16_07_05_53.pdf

Regulations Lab. (2022). *What is the regulations lab?* Accessed Feb 18, 2022, from https://reglab.gov.ae/en/about

Statisa. (2020). *"Coronavirus (COVID-19) deaths worldwide per one million population as of November 18, 2020, by country".* Accessed Nov 25, 2021, from https://www.statista.com/statistics/1104709/coronavirus-deaths-worldwide-per-million-inhabitants/

Trowers & Hamlins. (2021). *Dubai law regulating family business ownership.* Accessed Dec 5, 2021, from https://www.trowers.com/insights/2020/september/dubai-law-regulating-family-business-ownership

Vargese, J. (2021, April 21). UAE: How did family businesses come about and how are they structured? *Gulf news.* Accessed Dec 13, 2021, from https://gulfnews.com/your-money/expert-columns/uae-how-did-family-businesses-come-about-and-how-are-they-structured-1.1619001837624

Luan Eshtrefi is an Associate Professor at the Keller Graduate School of Management, DeVry University, the United States. He teaches graduate courses in Business Economics and Global Perspectives on International Business. Dr. Eshtrefi has been teaching for nearly 20 years at the tertiary level and has worked both in the private sector and in the public sector in multiple locations, to include Dubai, United Arab Emirates, where he was faculty lead in teaching Entrepreneurship and Innovation at a public university. His research interests currently focus on international business and globalization and entrepreneurship education. He has authored and co-authored multiple articles in reputable international journals and multiple book chapters.

Family Business in Gulf Cooperation Council Countries (GCC): Toward the Future

Wassim J. Aloulou

Abstract Family business is still an important component of the GCC economies. It still significantly influences the indicators of these economies by the employment created and value and wealth generated. This chapter highlights the critical weight of the GCC family businesses according to main key observers. After presenting the profile of these businesses and outlining their main characteristics, the chapter sets the main challenges of family businesses in the region and identifies the most important opportunities to seize by them in the future to sustain their businesses. Some perspectives of research are advanced for scholars and practitioners. Since this chapter comes concluding the book on family businesses in the GCC, it is something of a proposal for future research on these businesses in such geographical areas.

1 Introduction

The Gulf Cooperation Council (GCC) is an organization of six oil and gas exporting countries among the fastest growing economies in the world mainly due to energy revenues. They built a common market to ease the movement of goods, services, and people. GCC citizens are free to work in different organizations in all member states. The GCC countries share common faith of Arabian and Islamic culture, values, and lifestyle. All of them are Muslim-majority states with a total population of more than 57 million inhabitants (GCCSTAT, 2021).

GCC countries share a common economic interest, and they are seeking to push the diversification of their economy away from oil, expand their wealth and put their economies on a path of sustainable prosperity as recommended by the World Economic Forum since 2008. During the last decade, the GCC developed ambitious strategies and programs for their development and announced their vision for the next 15 years (Alharthi, 2019). Any business with global aspirations and ambitions

W. J. Aloulou (✉)
Imam Mohammad Ibn Saud Islamic University, Riyadh, Saudi Arabia
e-mail: Wjaloulou@imamu.edu.sa

© The Author(s), under exclusive license to Springer Nature Switzerland AG 2023
V. Ramadani et al. (eds.), *Family Business in Gulf Cooperation Council Countries*, Contributions to Management Science,
https://doi.org/10.1007/978-3-031-17262-5_8

will see these countries as being collectively important and full of potential growth. This impressive growth seen since 2008 is consolidated by the increase in energy production sales allowing the GCC to invest heavily in social services (health, education, utilities, etc.) and (digital) infrastructure (routes, highways, hospitals, universities, schools, etc.) and in sovereign wealth funds for future generations. These countries are not only attracting a large spectrum of skilled/unskilled occupations for local citizens and expatriates but also, many foreign direct investors facilitating the establishment of their companies. The GCC succeeded to provide a solid foundation for future economic development but have struggled to diversify their economies (Kabbani & Ben Minoun, 2021).

In recent years, the Gulf countries have developed initiatives to empower their private sectors for better integration into their ongoing economic activities: agencies such as "Monshaa't," Saudi Arabia's Small and Medium Enterprise Authority; Qatar Development Bank, and Oman's Riyada as examples; free trade zones and economic cities to attract foreign direct investments with a full protected ownership (Dana et al., 2021; Dana et al., 2022; Santosdiaz, 2020).

The great improvement of the business and entrepreneurial ecosystem is noticeable in the GCC countries with a real effort of reducing burdensome laws and regulations for the establishment of new firms, protecting (minority) investors, attracting venture capital, digitalizing administrative procedures, gaining reputation in the financial, touristic, cultural, sportive, and industrial sectors (Ashri, 2019; Saleem, 2021; Aloulou & Al-Othman, 2021; Aloulou & Alarifi, 2022). The design of an entrepreneurial ecosystem in the GCC is always influenced by the culture of the region and its economic settings to drive innovation and entrepreneurship (Alanzi et al., 2022). The GCC countries are trying to build robust entrepreneurial ecosystems as part of their strategy of diversifying their economies. They are also trying to offer great opportunities to funds and startups (Malek, 2019).

Regarding the structure of family businesses in GCC countries, Saudi Arabia and UAE dominate the Top family businesses in the Middle East according to Forbes with, respectively, 36 and 21 family businesses (Forbes, 2021). The rest of GCC countries included businesses in Kuwait with 10 family-owned firms, Oman with 6, Bahrain and Qatar with 5 each.

These family businesses included in this ranking are characterized as follows: (1) they are passed down through at least one generation; (2) around 80% of them are dealers or agents for successful international brands and franchises (automotive, fashion, and fast-moving consumer goods such as food and drink) (Al-Ubaydli, 2020; Forbes, 2021). The advantage of GCC family businesses is their ability to capture the region's significant growth via international partnerships, joint ventures, and franchises across multiple sectors. They have successfully transitioned from local trading businesses (merchants) to global multinationals (Issac, 2015; Palaiologos & Al Khunaizi, 2017; Al Awadi & Koster, 2017).

Recent reports confirmed that family businesses have become an important pillar of the national economy in many countries of the world, and especially in GCC countries. They continue to play a prominent role in the GCC region's impressive economic resilience and strength. Accounting for 70–80% of the entire regional private sector, they are considered as the backbone of the GCC economies by collectively generating US$ 100 billion in annual revenues and generating substantial employment opportunities for citizens (Orient Planet Group, 2017; Ulrichsen, 2017; Ahmad & El Agamy, 2021; Darwish et al., 2020; Deloitte &Touche, 2014). They make up the largest sector of the GCC economy and the second biggest investor after the government (Deloitte &Touche, 2014; Orient Planet Group, 2017). According to Alghanim (2021) and Ahmad and El Agamy (2021), family businesses are the private sector, with their economic success directly linked to the prosperity of the GCC region. It is estimated that 90% of the private sector in the United Arab Emirates (UAE) and Saudi Arabia consists of family-owned businesses. They contribute about 60% of the gross domestic product in the GCC and employ more than 80% of its labor force (Darwish et al., 2020). In short, family businesses in the GCC are economic powerhouses (Orient Planet Group, 2017). Over the last two decades, most of these family businesses are large conglomerates, holdings, or groups held by rich families (Zain & Kassim, 2012). They served and are still serving their communities and markets and are notable contributors to social causes in the GCC society (Davis et al., 2000; Buheji, 2017).

The chapter is structured as follows: First, the chapter presents a brief profiling of the GCC family businesses. Second, it identifies the main challenges that these businesses face. Third, it presents some opportunities that these businesses can seize for better and sustainable performance. Fourth, it opens some perspectives for research in the GCC family business field. In the end, it concludes by making a call for a scholarship to launch a series dedicated to family business in the GCC and deepen the understanding of complex phenomena related to it.

2 Profiling Family Businesses in the GCC

According to the GCC family survey conducted by McKinsey & Company in collaboration with the Gulf Family Business Council (GFBC) in 2014 (McKinsey & Company, 2015), the profile of the family businesses surveyed is shown as follows:

- They represented many of the largest businesses from across the GCC.
- They are relatively young; between 40 and 60 years old.
- Three-quarters of the businesses are run by the first or second generation.
- They collectively generate $100 billion in annual revenues across the region.
- More than 50% of the businesses have 5 or fewer shareholders.
- All businesses have at least one family member employed full-time in the business.
- Sixty percent of the businesses have 6 or more family members working in the business.
- Most of the businesses have diversified significantly within their home markets.

مجلــس الشركــات
العائليــة الخليجيــة

FAMILY BUSINESS COUNCIL-GULF

عضو في Member of FBN

Exhibit 1 Logo of the Family Business Council-Gulf (FBC-G). FBC-G is a private, nonprofit membership organization that aims to strengthen family business governance and ensure their continuity over generations, while learning from and where applicable adopting international best practices. Through research, education and capacity development, and networking among peers, the council seeks to identify and address issues that are unique to this region. Source: https://fbc-gulf.org/en/home

- Eighty-eight percent of businesses are present in 5 or more sectors, most common being real estate, construction, retail, manufacturing, and travel and leisure.
- Seventy-six percent of businesses have a presence outside of GCC.
- More than half of GCC's family businesses are in the midst of the transition from the second to third generation.

This profiling is aimed at understanding the health of family businesses in the region, their potential and characteristics related to generation, family ownership, and family members' involvement in management and control. No recent survey was conducted since that time (Exhibit 1).

In recent research, Darwish et al. (2020) make an update on the GCC family businesses' profile by suggesting that a family business' average lifespan in the region is only 23 years, compared to the 40 or 50 for today's multinational, Fortune 500 companies.

The single feature of a GCC family firm is the ownership structure. This structure takes the form of direct and complete family control by a handful of senior family members to influence the decision-making and adopt a long-term view (Raghu et al., 2016). The collectivist culture and larger size of families in the Arab world may be the primary reason why more family members own more shares in UAE family businesses than in family businesses in the rest of the world (Basco et al., 2020).

Under radical transformation of the world, family businesses worldwide and in the GCC region are facing many challenges in their field. These transformations may threaten their ability to compete and their survival. These conditions will force them to scale their businesses, improve their performance and attract new competent talents. They are invited to manage the critical transition phase and its difficulties for the second/third generation (Al-Barghouthi, 2016; Buheji, 2017). Some of them may not survive transition plans (Al Ghurair, 2015) or leadership contingency plans (Issac, 2015).

Over the past 2 years, family businesses face a unique set of challenges compounded by the economic disruption and technological transformation accelerated by the coronavirus pandemic. Such a challenge revealed to the world how family firms respond to a crisis to secure their continuity, ensure the safety of employees, and the engagement of stakeholders to find common solutions (Ahmad & Al agamy, 2021).

Sustaining the family business in GCC is imperative to ensure growth and longevity for generations to come during disruptive times. Four pillars of growth are covered according to a report of PwC (2019) when surveying family business in the middle east: setting the right foundation to attract and retain talents and develop a good governance and succession plans; creating a sustainable business by defining a strategy for the long term and optimizing the business portfolio; innovating and digitalizing by embracing new business models and investing in digital transformation; and looking outwards to be part of a fostering ecosystem to cope with regulations, collaborate with others and responsibly preserve the family business for the benefit of all. After the COVID-19 pandemic, family businesses are transforming for a sustainable future by setting their priorities for the next 2 years. There will be entrepreneurial actions to undertake such as expanding into new markets/client segments; increasing the use of new technologies; improving their digital capabilities; introducing new products and services; rethinking, changing, and adapting their business models (PwC, 2021b). For instance, GCC family businesses will be concerned by these challenges and reinforce their resilience amidst this pandemic (Orient Planet Group, 2020).

3 Main Challenges of Family Business in the GCC Region

Family businesses in the GCC face many challenges in order to maintain the legacy for the future generations. First, they must prepare adequate succession planning and appropriate transitioning to avoid conflicts with family members, owners, leaders, and shareholders. Second, they need to adopt a corporate governance that can help to sustain the legacy of their businesses over time. These issues remain critical to their competition in a globalized business setting (Stanhope, 2018; At Kearney, 2016). These two main challenges (succession and governance) are the solid fundamentals of the family business theory (Palaiologos & Al Khunaizi, 2017). Furthermore, new rules of engagement were set up by family businesses some years ago to sharpen up their acts in response to an intensified competition (Knowledge Wharton, 2010).

3.1 Succession Planning and Appropriate Transitioning to Avoid Family and Generational Conflicts

Succession is arguably one of the most critical issues a family business has to face and is also the most difficult aspect to plan for (Al Ghurair, 2016). Many are unprepared for the transition and did not have efficient assessment tools in place to identify positions and responsibilities for the next generation (Sabi, 2015).

It is considered as a big issue and painful one by scholars and practitioners facing the GCC family businesses (Annuar, 2019; Arabian Business, 2017; Ekanem & Alrossais, 2017; Palliam et al., 2011; Sabi, 2015). These businesses are representing about 60% of regional GDP and the transition of US$1 trillion will pass from generation to generation. In some GCC countries, family businesses are entering the third generation. According to Stanhope (2018), Raghu et al. (2016) and Buheji (2017), only about 45% of family businesses last until the first generation, only 30% of families manage to transition businesses to the second generation and one to ten makes it to the third generation successfully and less than 5% for the fourth generation. Some others failed to manage the transition because of the founder patriarch's concerns (death, getting old, etc.), the structures already being in place for legacy planning, new leadership, number of family shareholders grown from generation to the next, wealth built inside and outside the country, and compliance legacies. Passing a business from one generation to the next may affect the solid family bond and result in breaking it (Al Ghurair, 2016; Al-Saadi, 2017; Raghu et al., 2016). The choice of a competent successor is another challenge faced by any family business and put the founder(s) under pressure. Founders must establish a clear outline of the leadership of the business that will be passed to the next generation.

The succession challenge hides a legal challenge for family businesses consisting of how to separate between management and ownership. These two aspects are overlapped and can threaten the business sustainability (Alsharif, 2019). Successful family businesses are investing in their leadership from within the family to ensure the long-term continuity of the business (KPMG, 2018).

The lack of organization and legal structures in the business may impede the family business growth. A set of concrete recommendations were provided on the need to strengthen the legal framework that best fits the family succession planning across the GCC and support generational transfer of assets to ensure the growth and sustainability of their businesses (Augustine, 2015; Raghu et al., 2016). Furthermore, succession and inheritance issues should be addressed thoroughly by planning for succession through Fiqh (Islamic jurisprudence) and Sharia-based inheritance rules (Al-Barghouthi, 2016; Stanhope, 2018).

Generational conflicts are also decisive factors to be considered in any succession planning. To avoid such conflicts, family businesses must develop and enact a long-term strategy to manage both the interests and the intertwined culture of the family members with the business. The nature of the firm and its large size in the GCC puts pressure on family businesses to grow as quickly as possible to sustain the needs of various individual family units (Abu Bakar et al., 2015).

3.2 Corporate Family Governance

Family businesses in GCC must change their corporate governance to face their current challenge of succession for the next generation. Corporate and family governance is also a key issue that needs to be addressed as most of GCC family businesses have few formal procedures to deal with issues of control and ownership, and with the growing number of family shareholders from generation to the next, with a rising variety of member of the family in each generation, and with the expanding size of the company (siblings of the same mother, or of other mothers to different cousins, etc.) (Darwish et al., 2020; Raghu et al., 2016). As consequence, family conflicts can potentially increase. Additionally, most of the family businesses have not fully adopted modern global corporate cultures (Orient Planet Research, 2017). For larger family businesses that have reached the second or the third generation, the practice of management and control with separate boards has become an urgent matter (AlRebdi & Mohamad, 2021). In the UAE, findings show that large family businesses are more aware of transition failure and have long-term planning for their future generations in place than medium-sized family businesses (Oudah et al., 2018).

A second challenge regarding corporate and family governance is related to the legislation that supposes to govern the family businesses. For example, in Bahrain, there are big concerns and calls for binding legislation on family business governance to guarantee its continuity (Al-Barghouthi, 2016). However, in Saudi Arabia, a new Companies Law is recently issued to enable the conclusion of a family charter that regulates family ownership in the family business, its governance and management, work policy, employment of family members, and distribution of profits (Saudi Gazette, 2022). In the UAE, a legislative revolution is made by the creation of the Family Ownership Law that allows the setting out of the rights and responsibilities of family members (Alghanim, 2021; Al Awadi & Koster, 2017).

Corporate governance is crucial for family firms and lays the foundation for them to be more accountable and transparent in their operations which leads to a better future. First, having a strong well-functioning board of directors is important to act as intermediary between the family and the business. Second, defining clear responsibilities between family shareholders and the board, and between the board and the executive management is important too! Third, providing clear guidelines for employing qualified family and non-family members and impartial performance-based promotion is essential for the sustainability of the business (Williams, 2014).

4 Opportunities in GCC Family Businesses

In response to the abovementioned challenges, GCC family businesses have to seize many opportunities in their internal and external environments to secure long-term success and growth, enhance transparency, efficiency, and access to capital and talent, formalize management structures; and improve rules and processes.

4.1 Going Public with an Initial Public Offering

Going public is a key solution to ownership succession challenge in order to raise prompt and immediate cash flow, which can be later utilized for growing the business (Orient Planet Group, 2017; (Knowledge Wharton, 2010). A well-executed IPO can provide a way for the next generation to take over the business in an orderly manner, with less internal conflict. The family business become a publicly traded company and gain in visibility in its market and in accessibility to a wide range of investors. To succeed this IPO, the family business must be prepared and equipped with the necessary tools of due diligence. In the GCC region, there is a growing interest among family businesses to go public (Abbes, 2020; Al Awadi & Koster, 2017).

4.2 Role of Women in GCC Family Businesses

GCC family businesses have an opportunity to leverage a critical source of potential advantage: the women of the family (Strategy&, 2014). Women's participation and involvement in management, corporate governance, and succession plans can reinforce both family and business perspectives.

In the past, women have faced historically cultural obstacles to participation in the family business and their involvement in top management positions due to the cultural perceptions of a patriarchal society, a misalignment between the requirement of the business and the women's skills, or a situation of under-skilled women comparing to highly skilled men. For example, 5% of all family business boards in Bahrain are women (Al-Barghouthi, 2016). Recently, there is a supportive environment for GCC family businesses to take advantage of the contribution that their women can make (TradeArabia News, 2015; Majdalani et al., 2015; Arabian Business, 2017; Orient Planet Group, 2017). The GCC governments provide career opportunities to women who are well educated, empowered, and who are ready to take over leadership of their family business (Deloitte, 2019).

4.3 Leveraging the Next Generation

A well preparation next generation for the succession helps the family business to sustain its activities. Any delay in this succession means a lack of trust from the older generation in their abilities to lead the business and consequently, a lack of confidence of the next generation in themselves to act and face the challenges. Family business leaders must build confidence of the family in the upcoming successor. Family businesses need to act quickly to ensure their legacy in the future (PwC, 2021a).

According to a survey conducted by Deloitte (2019), helping the next generation to understand the business is considered as among the three highest priorities of respondents after their hope to continue family legacy and tradition and to preserve family capital.

Since most of the family businesses in the GCC region are reaching the critical stage of succession, they must rely on the next generation to provide them with ways to learn and work in the business.

5 Research Perspective on GCC Family Business

Family businesses have the potential to build a sustainable competitive advantage in the twenty-first century and to become better employers and more committed members of their communities (Baron, 2016; Baron & Lachenauer, 2021). They are likely to care about the economic and social rationales. All people involved in these businesses have the responsibility to sustain them.

The topic of family businesses in the GCC is not well documented and little literature was found dealing with the family businesses in the GCC countries. The literature is fragmented and scattered. This indicates that this research field is still in its infancy. To evolve and develop, this literature needs scholars and researchers to not talk to one another but communicate and connect with others (Zahra & Sharma, 2004). Although conferences and forums are regularly organized in the region,[1] little related documentation, exploratory in its nature, exists or is available to the scientific community. Future research needs to move toward more depth in understanding family business-based phenomena.

There is an urgent call from scholars to develop intensively interesting research questions on family businesses in the Arab world in general (Krueger et al., 2021) and in the Middle East in particular (Samara, 2021), communicate about them (Zahra & Sharma, 2004). For example, Krueger al. (2021) focus on family businesses in the Arab world to exemplify the benefits of better contextualizing family business research to further our understanding of heterogeneities among family businesses from diverse regions. So, contextualizing Family Business in the GCC countries means using a context-sensitive approach to recognize how context shapes the family business behavior and performance.

According to Zahra (2011) and Samara (2021), there is an accentuation of the GCC as a particular institutional setting (being a mixture of formal and informal variables) that offers opportunities to advance the family firm research. There is also an urgent call to understand the phenomenon of family business in the GCC countries for their potentiality and regional development impacts. Like Samara (2021), there is a way to think about making systematic literature reviews on GCC family businesses to organize knowledge about family business roles, family

---

[1] http://gulffamilybusiness.com/ as an example.

dynamics, family legacy and values transfer, family ownership, board dynamics, succession, generational differences, strategy, entrepreneurial and organizational behavior, governance, human resources, competitive advantage and performance, and social and economic impacts.

Family businesses in GCC countries are constituting an heterogenous population. This population contains different categories of businesses: listed vs. non listed; large vs. SME vs. small business, etc. Future research needs to deepen the understanding of each category and make comparisons between them (Neubaum et al., 2019).

We expedite the growth of research on GCC family businesses toward a better understanding of the following topics [2]:

1. Improving the understanding of the mechanisms of succession and governance in GCC family businesses.
2. Identifying the role of national culture of each country on these mechanisms.
3. Investigating the effects of Institutions (formal vs. informal) on the adoption of sustainable business practices in family businesses.
4. Exploring the family embeddedness in the next generations' entrepreneurial behavior.
5. Digitalization of family businesses and its effects on their professionalization.
6. Considering the resilient leadership of family businesses amidst the COVID-19 pandemic, etc.

We encourage scholars from the GCC countries to engage in the adoption of more rigorous theoretical and methodological choices to better understand the family business phenomenon.

6 Concluding Remarks

This chapter attempted to synthesize the most important facts on family businesses in the GCC region. The businesses are facing challenges and issues related to the succession planning process; conflict management and corporate governance; concentrated ownership and control; generational changes; wealth management and minority shareholders' rights. The chapter highlighted what we believe to be some potential opportunities for future research on family businesses in this area. In the end, the chapter concludes by making a call for scholarship to launch a series dedicated to family business in the GCC and deepen the understanding of complex phenomena related to it. Producing books of insightful case studies on family businesses in the GCC region will be of help for universities, educators, and students to diffuse family business culture among young people. These case studies, if developed according to the state-of-the art, will capture, and grasp the very unique

---

[2] The list is not exhaustive.

features and dimensions of family business in the region and their mechanisms and processes deployed in their activities (De Massis & Kotlar, 2014).

References

Abbes, W., (2020). More IPOs likely in GCC this year, but will not surpass value, *Khaleej Times*. Available at: https://www.khaleejtimes.com/local-business/more-ipos-likely-in-gcc-this-year-but-will-not-surpass-value

Abu Bakar, A. R. A., Ahmad, S. Z., & Buchanan, F. R. (2015). Trans-generational success of family businesses. *Journal for International Business and Entrepreneurship Development, 8*(3), 248–267.

Ahmad, A., & El Agamy, F. E., (2021). Family businesses in the Gulf must not be left behind, *Atlantic council*. Available at: https://www.atlanticcouncil.org/blogs/menasource/family-businesses-in-the-gulf-must-not-be-left-behind/

Al-Barghouthi, S. J. (2016). Passing the torch, family business succession, case study, Bahrain. *International Journal of Business and Management Studies, 5*(1), 279–294.

Al-Saadi, F. (2017, January 13). *Family disputes threaten the survival of family businesses in the Gulf*, Asharq Al-Awsat Newspaper. https://aawsat.com/home/article/829041/«-تهدد-استمرارية- الشركات-العائلية-في-الخليج-الخلافات-الأسرية».

Al-Ubaydli, O., (2020). Adapt and overcome: Gulf family businesses need to evolve to survive, *Alrabiya news*. Available at: https://english.alarabiya.net/views/news/middle-east/2020/07/12/Adapt-and-overcome-Gulf-family-businesses-need-to-evolve-to-survive

Al Ghurair, A (2015). 15% of GCC family firms may not survive transition plans. *Arabian business*. Available at: http://www.arabianbusiness.com/15-of-gcc-family-firms-may-not-survive-transition-plans-608913.html

Al Ghurair, A (2016, June 15). GCC family business succession a ticklish issue, *Saudi Gazette*. Available at: https://saudigazette.com.sa/article/157189/GCC-family-business-succession-a-ticklish-issue

Alanzi, S., Ratten, V., D'Souza, C., & Nanere, M. (2022). Culture, economic, and entrepreneurial environment in the Gulf cooperation council (GCC) countries. In V. Ratten (Ed.), *Strategic entrepreneurial ecosystems and business model innovation* (pp. 61–74). Emerald Publishing Limited. https://doi.org/10.1108/978-1-80382-137-520221005

Al Awadi, W. S., & Koster, H. (2017). *Corporate governance and sustainability of family businesses in the UAE*. Available at SSRN 3084378.

Alghanim, O. (2021). The family way: How the Gulf could create a more sustainable private sector, *CEO Middle East*. Available at: https://www.ceo-middleeast.com/innovation/463156-how-the-gulf-could-could-create-more-sustainable-private-sector

Alharthi, M. (2019). Determinants of economic development: A case of gulf cooperation council (GCC) countries. *International Journal of Economics and Finance, 11*(11), 12–18.

Aloulou, W. J., & Al-Othman, N. (2021, November). Entrepreneurship in Saudi Arabia. In L.-P. Dana, V. Ramadani, & R. Palalic (Eds.), *Entrepreneurship in GCC*. World Scientific Publishing. https://doi.org/10.1142/12082

Aloulou, W. J., & Alarifi, M. (2022). The context of business in Saudi Arabia. In L.-P. Dana, V. Salamzadeh Ramadani, & R. Palalic (Eds.), *Understanding contexts of business in Western Asia. Land of bazaars and high-tech booms* (pp. 477–494). World Scientific. https://doi.org/10.1142/9789811229695_0022

AlRebdi, A., & Mohamad, K. A. (2021). Unsustainable family business in Saudi Arabia-the roadmap ahead. *International Journal of Business and Management Research, 9*(2), 233–243.

Alsharif, D.T. (2019). *In Saudi Arabia, business runs in the family*. Available online at: https://www.arabnews.com/node/1579676

Annuar, N., (2019). The pains of succession planning in GCC family businesses, interviewing Daniel Fleming, Head of Wealth Advisory, Middle East at JP Morgan Private Bank. *Zawya*. Available at: https://www.zawya.com/en/wealth/the-pains-of-succession-planning-in-gcc-family-businesses-xuosb6xk

Arabian Business. (2017, April 22). *Governance, succession issues still hound GCCC family firms*. Available online: http://www.arabianbusiness.com/governance-succession-issues-still-hound-gcc-family-firms%2D%2D671120.html

Ashri, O. M. (2019). *On the fast track: Saudi Arabia's entrepreneurship ecosystem*. Available at: https://www.entrepreneur.com/article/336766

Augustine, B (2015). New impetus for GCC family business continuity. *Gulf news*. http://gulfnews.com/business/economy/new-impetus-for-gcc-family-business-continuity-1.1499715

Baron, J. (2016). Why the 21st century will belong to family businesses. *Harvard Business Review*, (March 28). Available at: https://hbr.org/2016/03/why-the-21st-century-will-belong-to-family-businesses

Baron, J., & Lachenauer, R. (2021). *Harvard business review family business handbook: How to build and sustain a successful*. Harvard Business Press.

Basco, R., Omari, Y., & Abouchkaier, L. (2020). *Family business ecosystem in United Arab Emirates. Family business in the Arab world observatory*. American University of Sharjah.

Buheji, M. (2017). Inspiring GCC family business towards lean governance: A comparative study with Japanese FB'S. *International Journal of Economics, Commerce and Management, 5*(7), 75–88.

At Kearney. (2016). *Family business in the GCC: Putting your house in order*, 12p. Available at: https://silo.tips/downloadFile/family-business-in-the-gcc-putting-your-house-in-order-improve-governance-refocu

Dana, L. P., Palalic, R., & Ramadani, V. (Eds.). (2021). *Entrepreneurship in the Gulf cooperation council region: Evolution and future perspectives*. World Scientific.

Dana, L. P., Salamzadeh, A., Ramadani, V., Palalić, R., & (Eds.). (2022). *Understanding contexts of business in Western Asia: Land of bazaars and high-tech booms*. World Scientific Publishing.

Darwish, S., Gomes, A., & Bunagan, V. (2020). Family business (FBS) in gulf cooperation council (GCC): Review and strategic insights. *Academy of Strategic Management Journal, 19*(3), 1–13.

Davis, J. A., Pitts, E. L., & Cormier, K. (2000). Challenges facing family companies in the Gulf region. *Family Business Review, 13*, 217–238.

De Massis, A., & Kotlar, J. (2014). The case study method in family business research: Guidelines for qualitative scholarship. *Journal of Family Business Strategy, 5*(1), 15–29.

Deloitte & Touche. (2014). *Deloitte: Family-owned businesses make up the largest sector of the GCC economy*. https://www2.deloitte.com/xe/en/pages/about-deloitte/articles/deloitte-family-owned-businesses-make-up-the-largest-sector-of-GCC-economy.html

Deloitte. (2019). Long-term goals, meet short-term drive. *Global family business survey*. Available at: https://www2.deloitte.com/content/dam/Deloitte/global/Documents/Strategy/gx-family-business-nextgen-survey.pdf

Ekanem, I., & Alrossais, L. A. (2017). Succession challenges facing family businesses in Saudi Arabia. In *Entrepreneurship and business innovation in the Middle East* (pp. 122–146). IGI Global.

Forbes. (2021, May). Top 100 Arab Family Businesses in the Middle East. *Forbes online*. Available at: https://www.forbesmiddleeast.com/lists/top-100-arab-family-businesses-in-the-middle-east-2021/

GCCSTAT. (2021–2022, November). *GCC Statistical Atlas 2021*. Volume 6. Available at: https://www.gccstat.org/en/center/docs/publications/2112-gcc-atlas-2021/file

Issac, J. (2015). Family businesses face key challenges in Middle East, *Khaleej Times*. Available at: https://www.khaleejtimes.com/local-business/family-businesses-face-key-challenges-in-middle-east

Kabbani, N., & Ben Minoun, N. (2021). *Economic diversification in the Gulf: Time to redouble efforts, Brookings Doha Center, report*. Available at: https://www.brookings.edu/wp-content/uploads/2021/01/Economic-diversification-in-the-Gulf.pdf

Knowledge Wharton. (2010, December 28). *Family firms in the Middle East: The new rules of engagement*. https://knowledge.wharton.upenn.edu/article/family-firms-in-the-middle-east-the-new-rules-of-engagement/

KPMG. (2018, February). *GCC family business survey 2017, Driving the region forward*, kpmg.com/familybusiness. Available at: https://assets.kpmg.com/content/dam/kpmg/sa/pdf/2017/6/GCC%20Family%20Business%20Survey%202017%20final%20DIGITAL%20low%20res.pdf?logActivity=true

Krueger, N., Bogers, M. L., Labaki, R., & Basco, R. (2021). Advancing family business science through context theorizing: The case of the Arab world. *Journal of Family Business Strategy, 12*(1), 100377.

Malek, C. (2019, December 23). *The great GCC entrepreneurial race*. How GCC countries are spurring entrepreneurship, Arab News, Monday. Available at: https://www.arabnews.com/sites/default/files/userimages/20/page3_61.pdf

Majdalani, F., Sfeir, S., Nader, P., & Omair, B. (2015). Women–the vital resource GCC family businesses should build upon. *The national News, business*. Available at: https://www.thenationalnews.com/business/women-the-vital-resource-gcc-family-businesses-should-build-upon-1.84798

McKinsey & Company. (2015, October). *Family Businesses in the Gulf Cooperation Council. The journey to long–term sustainability*. Available at: https://fbc-gulf.org/mediafiles/articles/doc-1362-20171117034009.pdf

Neubaum, D. O., Kammerlander, N., & Brigham, K. H. (2019). Capturing family firm heterogeneity: How taxonomies and typologies can help the field move forward. *Family Business Review, 32*(2), 106–130.

Orient Planet Group. (2017). *Family matters: Managing the GCC's family business powerhouses*. https://www.opresearch.me/reportDetails.aspx?id=132

Orient Planet Group. (2020, September). *Resilient leadership: navigating COVID-19 impact on GCC businesses*. Available at: https://www.opresearch.me/FreeReports.html

Oudah, M., Jabeen, F., & Dixon, C. (2018). Determinants linked to family business sustainability in the UAE: An AHP approach. *Sustainability, 10*, 246.

Palaiologos, G. T., & Al Khunaizi, Z. (2017). Growing the Arab family business (1): Hybrid organizational arrangements. *Journal of Entrepreneurship and Business Innovation, 4*(1), 25–46.

Palliam, R., Cader, H. A., & Chiemeke, C. (2011). Succession issues among family entrepreneurs in countries of the gulf. *International Journal of Business Administration, 2*, 25.

PwC. (2021a). *Family Business Survey 2021. From trust to impact*. Why family businesses need to act now to ensure the legacy tomorrow. Available at: https://www.pwc.com/gx/en/family-business-services/family-business-survey-2021/pwc-family-business-survey-2021.pdf

PwC. (2021b). *Diversifying, investing and digitising–Family businesses are transforming for a sustainable future*. Retrieved from https://www.pwc.com/m1/en/publications/family-business-survey/2021/documents/middle-east-family-business-survey-2021.pdf

PwC. (2019). *Future-proofing Middle East family businesses–Achieving sustainable growth during disruptive times*. Available at: https://www.pwc.com/m1/en/publications/documents/family-business-survey-2019.pdf

Raghu, M. R., Karthik Ramesh, N. C., & Lakshminarasimhan, N., (2016). *GCC family business. Continuing the success*. Marmore Industry Report. Available at: https://www.marmoremena.com/download.php?file=https://www.marmoremena.com/wp-content/uploads/pdfnew/1591181181_GCC%20Family%20Business%20-%20Executive%20Summary%20-%20Marmore%20Research%20Report.pdf

Sabi, A. (2015). *The succession challenge in GCC family businesses, Global Risk Insights.* Available at: https://globalriskinsights.com/2015/11/the-succession-challenge-in-gcc-family-businesses/

Saleem, I. (2021). A Strategy for Family Business Survival during the Crisis in Gulf Business Environment. *Academia Letters*, 2.

Samara, G. (2021). Family businesses in the Arab Middle East: What do we know and where should we go? *Journal of Family Business Strategy, 12*(3), 100359. https://doi.org/10.1016/j.jfbs.2020.100359

Santosdiaz, R. (2020). *Overview of the economic development strategies in the Middle East's GCC Region.* Available at: https://thefintechtimes.com/overview-of-the-economic-development-strategies-in-the-middle-easts-gcc-region/

Saudi Gazette. (2022). *Saudi Arabia's new companies' law highly flexible, embraces international best practices.* Available at: https://saudigazette.com.sa/article/622367/SAUDI-ARABIA/Saudi-Arabias-new-companies-law-highly-flexible-embraces-international-best-practices

Stanhope, M., (2018). Family businesses in the GCC–the challenges they face, Hubbis. *Middle East Wealth Management Forum.* Available at: https://pdf.hubbis.com/pdf/article/family-businesses-in-the-gcc-the-challenges-they-face.pdf

Strategy&. (2014). *Leveraging an untapped talent pool: How to advance women's role in GCC family businesses.* Alsayedah Khadijah Bint Khuwailid Center. Available at: https://www.ioe-emp.org/fileadmin/ioe_documents/publications/Policy%20Areas/gender/EN/_2016-09-26__Strategy_AKBK_Leveraging_an_untapped_talent_pool.pdf

TradeArabia News. (2015, January 20). *Women to take more active roles in GCC firms.* http://www.tradearabia.com/news/EDU_273749.html

Ulrichsen, K. C. (2017). Economic Diversification in Gulf Cooperation Council (GCC) States. *Center of Energy Studies,* Houston, TX: Rice University.

Williams, A. (2014). *Corporate governance is the key GCC family business groups need to unlock full potential. Pedersen & Partners.* Available at: https://www.pedersenandpartners.com/news/corporate-governance-key-gcc-family-business-groups-need-unlock-full-potential

Zahra, S. A. (2011). Doing research in the (new) Middle East: Sailing with the wind. *The Academy of Management Perspectives, 25*(4), 6–21.

Zahra, S. A., & Sharma, P. (2004). Family business research: A strategic reflection. *Family Business Review, 17*(3), 331–346.

Zain, M., & Kassim, N. M. (2012). Strategies of family businesses in a newly globalized developing economy. *Journal of Family Business Management, 2*(1), 147–165.

Wassim J. Aloulou is an Associate Professor at the College of Economics and Administrative Sciences at Imam Mohammad Ibn Saudi Islamic University, Riyadh, KSA. He received his PhD in Management Sciences from the University of Pierre Mendes, France Grenoble 2, France, and from the Faculté des Sciences Economiques et de Gestion de Sfax, Tunisia in 2008. He teaches graduate and undergraduate courses in entrepreneurship in MBA and BBA programs. His research interests currently focus on digital entrepreneurship, FinTech, entrepreneurial intentions, and orientations of individuals and organizations. He has authored and co-authored multiple articles in reputable international journals (e.g., *European Journal of Innovation Management, Journal of Small Business and Enterprise Development,* and *International Journal of Logistics Management*), books with IGI Global on business transformations and resilience, and multiple book chapters (with Edward Elgar and World Scientific).

Printed in the United States
by Baker & Taylor Publisher Services